THE ONE REALITY BRIEF

A Forensic Analysis of Aliens, AI, and the War for Dominion

By Scott M. Kendall, J.D.

The One Reality Brief: A Forensic Analysis of Aliens, AI, and the War for Dominion

Ox Barn Press, Las Vegas, Nevada

> *"Without oxen a stable stays clean, but you need a strong ox for a large harvest."* (Proverbs 14:4, NLT)

Disclaimer This book is a work of non-fiction. The events and conversations documented herein are true and accurate to the best of the author's recollection. Certain names and identifying details of incidental figures may have been altered to protect their privacy; however, the primary witnesses cited in the text have provided permission for their names and likenesses to be used.

Cataloging-in-Publication Data

Kendall, Scott M. The One Reality Brief: A Forensic Analysis of Aliens, AI, and the War for Dominion / Scott M. Kendall, J.D.

1. Unidentified Flying Objects—Religious aspects—Christianity. 2. Spiritual Warfare. 3. Artificial Intelligence—Religious aspects. 4. Bible—Prophecy. I. Title.

ISBN (eBook): 979-8-9950020-0-0 ISBN (Paperback): 979-8-9950020-1-7 ISBN (Hardcover): 979-8-9950020-2-4

First Edition: February 2026 Printed in the United States of America

Table of Contents

INTRODUCTION: THE OPENING STATEMENT

Picture yourself strapped into the cockpit of a B-52 Stratofortress, hurtling through ink-black night at four hundred knots. Zero visibility. Cloud layers thick as concrete swallow the horizon. Your instruments glow steady, but your body screams betrayal—vertigo twists the world, whispering that down is up, that a gentle climb is a fatal dive. Fear claws at the yoke: pull back, it urges, save yourself. One wrong move, one surrender to the lie of your senses, and the jet becomes a fireball. Survival demands a single, iron discipline: trust the radar. Ignore the feelings. Fly the instruments.

Now step into a courtroom, seventeen years of litigation etched into your bones. The witness swears to a story that tugs every heartstring—tears, tragedy, righteous outrage. But the rules of evidence are merciless. Hearsay dies on the floor. Rumor is inadmissible. Emotion is irrelevant. You build the case brick by brick: chain of custody, physical proof, corroborated testimony. You separate signal from noise until only truth remains standing, cold and unassailable.

For eighty years, humanity has been flying blind through a storm of High Strangeness, refusing both the radar and the rules.

Lights streak across the sky at impossible velocities, executing right-angle turns that shred physics textbooks. Craft materialize over nuclear silos, over oceans, over bedroom windows. Non-human entities—tall, short, grey, luminous—enter homes, paralyze occupants, leave radiation burns, scoop marks, implants. Poltergeist chaos erupts in their wake. Witnesses from ranchers to fighter pilots, from children to four-star generals, report the same impossible details. Yet our institutions—built to protect us—have failed the test.

The Pentagon, locked in a materialist fortress, stares at a craft out-accelerating our fastest jets without sonic boom or heat signature and declares it a machine. They hunt for propulsion, lift-to-drag ratios, foreign adversaries. They catalog the metal but ignore the mind—the telepathy that floods pilots' heads, the paralysis that pins bodies to beds, the poltergeist activity that follows contact home. Those details don't fit the secular spreadsheet, so they vanish from the briefing.

Across town, the Church peers at the same phenomenon through a theological keyhole and sees only demons—pure spirit, disembodied evil masquerading as lights in the sky. They recoil from the physical evidence: ground indentations baked into soil, radiation levels that hospitalize witnesses, biological implants removed under X-ray. Those traces don't fit the spiritual model, so they are dismissed as coincidence or deception.

This artificial wall between Science and Spirit—this Partition—has left us disoriented, arguing over shadows while the puppeteers move unchecked.

The Partition whispers a lie we have swallowed whole: the physical world and the spiritual world are separate rooms with no connecting door. If something is technological, it cannot be supernatural. If it is spiritual, it cannot leave fingerprints, radiation, or DNA.

This book is a forensic rebuttal to that deception.

I have spent my life in cockpits and courtrooms where a single miscalculation ends in catastrophe. As a B-52 Radar Navigator, I held a Top Secret ESI clearance, trained to safeguard the nation's most sensitive secrets while guiding multi-million-dollar bombers through hostile skies. As an attorney with seventeen years trying cases and arguing appeals, I learned to dismantle lies with evidence, not emotion. In both arenas, truth rarely hides in extremes. It emerges in synthesis—when you trust the instruments and follow the chain of custody.

The One Reality Brief is not speculation. It is an evidentiary filing.

We are not grappling with two unrelated mysteries—the "Alien" from the stars and the "Watcher" from ancient texts. We face one unified incursion: intelligences that are fully physical and fully spiritual at once. Beings who navigate quantum realms yet flee at the name of Jesus. Craft that mock gravity yet demand legal permission to trespass our domain.

In the pages ahead, we will prosecute the Silent Invasion with precision:

- We will map the Physics of the Dark Sector, revealing how these entities step through the curtain rather than cross the void.
- We will trace the Chain of Custody from ancient forges to Roswell debris, exposing the illicit cargo that built our digital prison.
- We will unmask the human collaborators—the Vichy Government of the modern age—rebranding terror as enlightenment.
- And finally, we will lay out the ancient Law of Dominion, the Title Deed that empowers humanity to serve the ultimate eviction notice.

The Partition is crumbling. Washington calls it Disclosure. The New Age heralds Ascension. The Bible names it the End of the Age.

Whatever label you choose, the wall is coming down. And on the other side stands the intelligence we have mistaken for gods, saviors, or mere anomalies.

It is time to trust the instruments.

It is time to face the fire.

It is time to see who has been pulling the strings all along.

Chapter 1: The Civil War

Plato's Prisoners and the Paralysis of State

Imagine a cave carved deep into living rock, lit only by a single fire burning somewhere behind you. You sit chained, neck fixed by iron links, eyes locked on a blank wall. Behind you—unseen—puppeteers carry cut-out figures: men, animals, tools, weapons. They pass between the fire and the wall. Shadows leap and twist across the stone. You name them. You argue over their shapes, their meanings, their hierarchy. You build philosophies, religions, entire civilizations around the flickering forms. You fight wars over which shadow is truest. You have never turned your head. You have never seen the fire. You have never known the world outside.

For the last eighty years, the most powerful intelligence apparatus in human history—the Pentagon—has been chained in exactly that cave.

The United States government possesses satellites that can read a license plate from orbit, submarines that glide silent beneath polar ice, radar networks that pierce the night from continent to continent. Yet when confronted with craft that accelerate from standstill to hypersonic in a heartbeat, that execute right-angle turns without deceleration, that descend into oceans and emerge without a ripple, the response has been paralysis. Not because of lack of data. Not because of budget constraints. Because of theology.

The intelligence community has fractured into two warring camps—two sets of prisoners staring at the same wall of shadows but seeing entirely different things.

The first camp sees machines.

The second sees monsters.

Neither will turn around to face the fire.

I. The Materialists: The Ghost of Jack Parsons

The Materialists are the engineers, the analysts, the physicists—the men and women who built the jet age and the space age. To them, the phenomenon is a hardware problem. A craft traveling at Mach 20 without a sonic boom? Must be an advanced propulsion system. No visible exhaust? Must be a breakthrough in lift-to-drag ratios. Telepathy? Paralysis? Poltergeist activity? Irrelevant noise. They want funding for wind tunnels, sensor arrays, materials testing. They want to reverse-engineer the machine.

But the irony cuts like a blade. The father of their own rocket program was not a materialist. He was a sorcerer.

In the 1940s, Jack Parsons stood at the intersection of fire and steel. A self-taught chemist with no formal degree, he co-founded the Jet Propulsion Laboratory as part of Caltech's GALCIT Rocket Research Group. He pioneered castable composite propellants and JATO units—solid-fuel boosters that gave bombers extra kick on takeoff. His work helped propel America to the Moon. By day, he was the architect of thrust and combustion, the man who turned barren desert test stands into launchpads, who watched flames roar and knew he was touching the future.

By night, in a sprawling Pasadena mansion known as the Parsonage on South Orange Grove Avenue, he was high priest of the Agape Lodge of the Ordo Templi Orientis—the California branch of Aleister Crowley's Thelemic order. The house was a commune of occultists, artists, and scientists. Rocket fuel mingled with incense. Engineering schematics lay beside magical grimoires. The air smelled of sulfur, cordite, and sex.

The most notorious chapter unfolded in early 1946: the Babalon Working. Parsons, with L. Ron Hubbard—then a young Navy veteran and aspiring writer—acting as his magical scribe, conducted a prolonged series of sex-magic rituals designed to tear open the veil between worlds. They invoked Enochian keys—the angelic language John Dee had received in the 16th century. They offered masturbatory libations onto inscribed tablets while Sergei Prokofiev's Second Violin Concerto played in the background. They chanted to summon elemental forces, believing they could incarnate the Thelemite goddess Babalon on Earth as a living Scarlet Woman who would birth a "moonchild"—a magical heir to usher in Crowley's prophesied new Aeon of Horus.

The ceremonies began in the temple room of the Parsonage: candles flickering, incense thick, bodies and invocations intertwined. The climactic phase shifted to the remote Mojave Desert. Under a vast, starlit sky in late February, Parsons performed a solitary sunset rite, convinced the goddess descended upon him. He declared the Working complete, certain the barriers of space and time had been breached.

Parsons drew no line between his scientific pursuits and his occult practices. To him, both were twin engines driving humanity toward godhood: the rocket as physical ascent through the atmosphere toward the stars; the ritual as metaphysical ascent to summon otherworldly powers and tear open doorways to higher realities. Engineering and evocation were complementary paths to transcendence.

The modern Materialist faction tries to bury this history. They want the science without the séance. They want to solve the puzzle of UAP while pretending their own founding father did not believe the beings were summoned rather than discovered. They stare at the shadow of the rocket, refusing to look at the fire of the ritual.

II. The Collins Elite: The Priest in the Pentagon

The second camp knows exactly who Jack Parsons was talking to. And they are terrified.

In 1991, Ray Boeche—an Anglican priest and former Nebraska State Director for MUFON—was contacted by two men from the Department of Defense. They arranged a clandestine meeting in Lincoln, Nebraska. These were not low-level clerks; they were physicists and intelligence officers working deep within the Pentagon's black programs. They laid a briefcase of documents on the table. They told Boeche a story that sounded like madness.

They claimed the U.S. government had recovered crashed saucers and bodies. But the "Aliens" were a lie. The entities were Non-Human Intelligences (NHI) of a strictly spiritual nature—demonic, the deceiving spirits of Scripture. Investigation was invocation. Sensors, communication attempts, even focused thought granted them permission to enter our reality.

This faction, later dubbed the Collins Elite, operates as a shadow government within the DIA and Air Force. Their worldview is not scientific; it is traditional biblical demonology. They view the entities as chaotic, evil spirits serving Satan. Their policy is simple: do not study. Bury it.

As former AATIP director Luis Elizondo recounts in his memoir *Imminent*, he faced constant obstruction from senior officials. One superior told him bluntly: "We already know what they are. They are demonic. And we should not be engaging them."

To the Collins Elite, the Materialists are not just wrong—they are spiritually naive fools unwittingly performing a mass occult ritual, opening a door to Hell they cannot close.

III. The Fatal Error: The False Dichotomy

This is the tragedy of the American response. The paralysis in Washington is not incompetence; it is the product of a fundamental ontological war.

The Secularist argues: "We need money to study the propulsion."

The Gatekeeper responds: "I am not authorizing money to summon demons."

Both are wrong. Both operate under the assumption of mutual exclusivity:

Premise A: If it is a nuts-and-bolts craft, it cannot be a spirit.

Premise B: If it is a spirit, it cannot be a nuts-and-bolts craft.

This is the error of the cave. They mistake the shadow for the object. The Materialist fails to see that the craft behaves like consciousness—telepathy, shapeshifting, observer-dependency. The Religious man fails to see that the demon leaves physical traces—radiation burns, ground indentations, biological implants.

The Bible makes no such distinction. Spiritual beings eat food (Genesis 18), engage in physical combat (Genesis 32), wield objects that manipulate matter (Exodus 7). The "spiritual" is simply a higher order of physics—a Super-Nature, not a Supernatural.

The real danger is not that one side will win. The danger is that both sides are unwittingly building the End Game.

The Materialists are constructing the hardware: AI, rockets, bio-engineering.

The Collins Elite are ignoring the software—the Entity—hoping it goes away.

Meanwhile, the Entity waits for the hardware to be finished so it can move in.

In the chapters that follow, we will do what the prisoners refuse to do. We will turn around. We will look away from the wall and stare directly at the fire. We will present the One Reality Brief—a unified theory that explains how the spiritual entity and the alien are the same creature, how the machine and the mark are the same trap.

We are not dealing with two mysteries.

We are dealing with one invasion.

Chapter 2: The Evolving Lexicon

Confession by Redefinition

In the world of law and intelligence, words are never neutral. They are boundaries. They are fences. They are weapons.

Tell a detective the crime is “burglary,” and he sweeps the scene for shattered glass, pry marks, footprints in the flowerbed. Tell him it’s “embezzlement,” and he never leaves the office—he opens ledgers, traces wire transfers, follows the money. The chosen word does not merely describe reality; it dictates where the flashlight points. Change the word, and the entire crime scene can vanish—or be rebuilt somewhere else entirely.

For seventy years, the United States government investigated the phenomenon in our skies using one carefully engineered term: **UFO**—Unidentified Flying Object.

That phrase was never innocent. It was a linguistic cage, built to trap a Soviet aircraft.

I. The Trap of the “Flying Object”

Washington, D.C.

July 19, 1952.

A sweltering Saturday night. Humidity so thick it clung to the tarmac at Washington National Airport like wet cloth. Inside the air traffic control center, the air conditioning wheezed against the heat.

At 11:40 p.m., controller Edward Nugent glanced at his radar scope. Seven bright blips materialized 15 miles south-southwest of the capital—sudden, unannounced, and moving in ways no scheduled flight ever would.

He called his supervisor, Harry Barnes. “Here they are,” Nugent said, voice low. “We have them.”

Barnes watched the targets dance: erratic speeds, abrupt direction changes, hovering, then explosive acceleration. No transponder codes. No flight plans. Three other controllers confirmed the returns. The tower at the airport saw the same thing—bright, hovering lights that departed at impossible velocity when fighters were scrambled.

F-94 Starfires roared out of New Castle, Delaware. Lt. William Patterson chased four glowing orbs that surrounded him, pulled away effortlessly, then vanished. Ground radar tracked the same dance: the objects appeared to monitor radio traffic, slipping away just as interceptors closed.

The sightings stretched until 5:30 a.m. They returned the following weekend. Headlines screamed. The nation watched the sky.

The government faced a public-relations catastrophe. They could not explain the lights, but they could not afford panic. In January 1953, the CIA convened the Robertson Panel—a closed-door gathering of physicists and astronomers. Their conclusion was chilling: the objects themselves might not be the threat, but the fear they inspired could be exploited by adversaries.

They recommended systematic debunking. Use mass media to ridicule witnesses. Reduce the subject to a punchline.

To enforce the policy, the Air Force codified the term **UFO**.

Do not overlook the engineering of that acronym.

- **Flying** — implies aerodynamics, lift, drag, thrust.

- **Object** — implies solid matter, nuts, bolts, hull.

The label was a psychological containment wall. As long as the phenomenon was a "flying object," every investigation remained safely terrestrial: foreign prototype, experimental aircraft, temperature inversion, Venus. High Strangeness—telepathy, paralysis, time distortion, biological effects—could be quietly shelved as psychological artifacts. The cage held.

The man charged with enforcing that cage was Dr. J. Allen Hynek, astronomer from Northwestern University and scientific consultant to Project Blue Book. For years he played the role faithfully: swamp gas, Venus, misidentified aircraft. But the data kept piling up. By the 1970s, Hynek's certainty cracked. He coined "Close Encounters," speculated openly that the phenomenon was not extraterrestrial but interdimensional—a reality that "interlocks" with our own.

Hynek became the first high-profile casualty of the lexicon he had helped enforce. He realized the words he was paid to use were a lie.

II. The Academic Betrayal: The Condon Committee

While Hynek wrestled with conscience, the Air Force sought a clean exit. The "UFO" label had become a political liability. They needed a scientific whitewash.

In 1966, they contracted the University of Colorado to conduct the definitive study. Physicist Edward Condon was appointed to lead it. To the public, it looked like the moment science would finally take the subject seriously.

It was a hit job.

Before the first witness was interviewed, project administrator Robert Low wrote a leaked memo outlining the real strategy:

“The trick would be to describe the project so that, to the public, it would appear a totally objective study, but to the scientific community would present the image of a group of nonbelievers trying their best to be objective, but having an almost zero expectation of finding a saucer.”

When the Condon Report appeared in 1968, the case files contained hundreds of unexplained incidents that defied conventional physics. Yet Condon’s summary ignored his own team’s data: “further extensive study of UFOs probably cannot be justified.”

The media read the summary, not the files. The New York Times declared the mystery solved. Project Blue Book was shuttered.

The linguistic trap was bolted shut. The Condon Report created the stigma. For the next fifty years, any scientist who uttered “UFO” risked funding. Any pilot who reported one risked his wings. The Materialists had successfully exiled the phenomenon to the tabloids. They stopped looking up.

And because they stopped looking, they didn’t notice when the “objects” changed tactics.

III. The “Anomalous” Pivot: The Death of the Object

The silence held until the hardware refused to behave like hardware.

July 15, 2019. USS Omaha, off the coast of San Diego. The Combat Information Center glows red. On the infrared feed: a perfect black sphere, six feet across, hovering motionless above the Pacific. No wings. No rotor. No exhaust.

Then it drops.

Physics demands a violent splash, thermal bloom, debris. The sphere slips through the surface tension like it isn't there. Submersibles search the seafloor. Nothing. No hull. No wreckage.

The Navy quietly documented one of the "Five Observables" codified by Luis Elizondo during AATIP:

1. Anti-gravity lift
2. Sudden acceleration
3. Hypersonic velocity
4. Low observability
5. Trans-medium travel

The fifth killed the "object" label. No machine built for air can plunge into water without resistance. No object can do all five. But an anomaly can.

In the 2023 National Defense Authorization Act, Congress quietly changed the scope:

Unidentified Aerial Phenomena → Unidentified Anomalous Phenomena

"Aerial" was dropped. The phenomenon no longer had to fly. It could move through air, water, and solid matter without obeying the rules of baryonic matter. The government legally admitted that Newtonian physics were being bypassed.

IV. The "Consciousness" Pivot: The Invisible College

The next shift addressed the observer. Condon had banned the study of the pilot's mind. If a witness claimed the object "spoke" to him, he was unstable.

But in the shadows, a group of high-level scientists—the Invisible College—began to realize the human element was central.

Project Stargate (1970s–1990s) had already shown the CIA that consciousness could be a sensor. Remote viewers like Ingo Swann described distant targets with uncanny accuracy—and frequently reported being noticed by "entities" during sessions. The government knew for decades that the mind could detect what radar could not. Condon's stigma buried it.

By the 2010s, the knowledge resurfaced. In *American Cosmic*, religious studies professor Diana Pasulka gained access to elite bio-engineers and crash-retrieval insiders. One guide—"Tyler," a NASA-affiliated scientist—drove her into the New Mexico desert to hunt artifacts. He fasted. He deprived himself of sleep. He entered a meditative state to "receive" the location of debris.

Pasulka watched atheists recreating the ascetic practices of Catholic saints—only they called it a "protocol."

Stanford pathologist Garry Nolan took it further. Studying the brains of high-functioning "Experiencers" (intelligence officers with close encounters), he found hyper-density in the caudate-putamen—the brain's intuition center. He theorized it acts as an "antenna," tuning into a signal present in the environment but invisible to most people.

The translation is unmistakable.

Theological view: A prophet receives visions through prayer and fasting.

Secular view: An experiencer receives downloads through a hyper-connected caudate-putamen and disciplined “protocols.”

The same phenomenon, stripped of moral weight and dressed in laboratory language.

V. The “Infection” Pivot: Secularizing the Demon

The most unsettling shift concerns the aftermath. Materialists want the craft to fly away. The data shows it often follows you home.

AAWSAP investigators tracked intelligence officers who visited active sites and brought “something” back to their families in Virginia and Maryland: shadows moving, orbs in hallways, voices in empty rooms.

The government coined a clinical term: **The Hitchhiker Effect**.

The translation is transparent.

Theological view: Demonic oppression. A person opens a door at a cursed place; a familial spirit attaches, harassing the household.

Secular view: Infectious cognitive agent. A person acquires an anomalous contagion at a site; it transmits along genetic lines.

The behavior is identical. Only the label protects the grant money.

VI. The “NHI” Pivot: The Legal Catch-All

In July 2023, former intelligence officer David Grusch testified before Congress. He deliberately avoided “extraterrestrial.” Instead he used **Non-Human Intelligence (NHI)**. When pressed on origin, he said: “I don’t want to necessarily denote origin.”

The term is a masterstroke. It encompasses anything intelligent that is not human—biological, interdimensional, spiritual—without forcing a materialist conclusion. It overlaps almost perfectly with the theological category of "spirit."

VII. The Verdict: A Soft Disclosure

The irony is complete.

The secular faction changed every term to make the study sound more scientific, to escape the giggle factor of "little green men." In doing so, they unintentionally confessed to the One Reality.

- "Dark Sector" is the secular map for the Unseen Realm.
- "Consciousness" is the secular word for spirit.
- "Hitchhiker Effect" is the secular diagnosis for oppression.

The "nuts and bolts" paradigm is dead. The "spirits" have returned, disguised as "anomalous phenomena." The government is finally admitting that we live in a universe teeming with invisible, intelligent life capable of manipulating our reality and our minds. They simply haven't admitted who that life is.

They have built a secular theological lexicon. They are describing a spiritual war in the language of quantum mechanics.

But changing the label does not change the lethality of the threat. A "Non-Human Intelligence" is just as dangerous as a demon—perhaps more so, because we have convinced ourselves it is neutral.

As we will see in the next chapter, this war is not confined to the skies or classified briefings. It is contagious. The phenomenon does not merely appear on radar. It attaches to the observer.

Chapter 3: The Smoking Gun

The Hitchhiker Effect

If the shift in government language (Chapter 2) was the confession, the Hitchhiker Effect is the smoking gun.

For eighty years, the prosecution of the phenomenon has been stalled by a hung jury. The intelligence community remains deadlocked between two irreconcilable verdicts:

- The Materialists insist these are "nuts-and-bolts" machines—and therefore cannot be spirits.
- The Mystics insist these are demons or ghosts—and therefore cannot be physical.

Both sides are wrong.

They are ignoring the literal blood on the floor: radiation burns, detached scalps, trajectory-specific cancers, and a contagion that follows investigators home to terrorize their children.

In 2009, the Defense Intelligence Agency deployed officers to Skinwalker Ranch in Utah. Those officers did not merely observe anomalies; they carried an infection back to their families in Virginia. It was investigative journalist George Knapp who first brought this contagion into public view, giving it the name that now defines the phenomenon: the **Hitchhiker Effect**.

This single data point is the most devastating evidence in the One Reality Brief. It destroys the Partition in one stroke.

A machine does not follow a scientist home and terrorize his children.

A hallucination does not leave radiation burns or cause rare cancers.

The Hitchhiker Effect forces a verdict that shatters every category: we are dealing with an intelligence that behaves simultaneously like a **virus** (contagious), a **demon** (oppressive), and a **nuclear reactor** (radioactive).

This is not a ghost story. It is a biological—and ontological—attack.

I. The Impossible Body: The Bulletproof Wolf

To understand why the old categories fail, we must start in the mud.

> 1994. The Uinta Basin, Utah. Terry and Gwen Sherman had just purchased a 512-acre cattle ranch. On one of their first days, under a low, drizzling sky, they watched a wolf approach the corral where a calf was penned.

The animal was enormous—shoulder height nearly matching a man's chest—its coat dark and glossy, its gait unnaturally calm. It moved with the deliberate grace of a predator that had never known fear.

The moment it struck, beauty turned to horror. The wolf lunged through the fencing, clamped its jaws on the calf's snout, and began dragging the screaming animal through the bars.

Terry Sherman did not hesitate. He drew a .357 Magnum—a revolver capable of stopping a grizzly—and fired into the wolf's ribs at point-blank range.

The result was forensic nonsense.

No spray of blood. No yelp. No stagger. The animal absorbed the impact without flinching. Sherman fired again. And again. Three rounds that should have shattered bone and shredded lung. The wolf simply released the calf, turned, stared at Sherman with cold, detached intelligence, and trotted away.

He tracked it across the wet field. The paw prints continued for several hundred yards—then stopped. No body. No blood trail. Nothing.

The Forensic Verdict:

- The Materialist cannot explain it. A biological animal bleeds when shot.
- The Mystic cannot explain it. A ghost or hologram cannot physically bite a calf and exert hundreds of pounds of drag force.

The bulletproof wolf is the first warning shot of the One Reality. We are dealing with a trans-substantial entity—capable of mass and force in our world, yet immune to our physics. It shattered the Partition in a muddy corral.

II. The Impossible Machine: The Kitchen Intrusion

While the Shermans faced a biological impossibility, the DIA faced a technological one.

2007. Dr. James Lacatski, a rocket scientist and DIA intelligence analyst, sat in the ranch house kitchen conducting a hard-nosed logistical assessment. He was there for data, not spirits.

The environment shifted without warning.

In the living room, suspended in mid-air, a complex structure materialized. Lacatski described it as a “techno-structure”—a Möbius-like ribbon of impossible geometry, composed of a dark, light-absorbing material that seemed to drink the ambient illumination. It had structure, form, deliberate intricacy. It was unmistakably a machine.

Yet it did not arrive through a door or window. It did not have propulsion. It simply appeared from empty air, hovered in menacing silence, and then dematerialized.

The Forensic Verdict:

Lacatski saw a machine that behaved like a ghost. This moment kills the "nuts-and-bolts" argument. If this were an extraterrestrial spacecraft, it would obey aerodynamics and conservation laws. Instead, it behaved like a projection—an intrusion from the Bulk rather than an arrival from another planet.

It proved that the "technology" we chase is not manufactured. It is conjured.

III. The Infection: The Axelrod Case

In conventional war, you leave the battlefield and you are safe. In spiritual war, the enemy follows you.

DIA officer "Axelrod" (Jay Stratton) visited the ranch in 2009. He completed his tour, gathered his data, boarded a commercial flight, and returned 2,000 miles to the suburbs of Northern Virginia. He assumed the event was over.

He was wrong. The entity had attached.

The horror began in his own backyard. His wife—unaware of the specifics of his assignment—saw a massive wolf-like creature staring at her from the edge of their garden. The same impossible biology seen in Utah.

But it did not stop with visuals.

The infection spread to his children. His teenage sons began experiencing severe sleep paralysis and night terrors. They saw blue orbs floating through the hallway of their home—the exact luminous anomalies recorded by sensors 2,000 miles away.

The Forensic Verdict:

- Against the Materialist: A “nut-and-bolt” craft cannot fly into your mind, travel via commercial airliner, and reappear in your garden.
- Against the Skeptic: A father’s stress does not cause his children to see specific blue orbs matching classified sensor data.

The Hitchhiker Effect is the secular diagnosis for what the Church has always called demonic oppression or familial spirits—except now it is documented in classified DIA files and leaves measurable physical traces.

This creates a terrifying legal precedent: **the investigation is the vector**. By merely observing the phenomenon, the officer formed a quantum entanglement with it, granting the entity permission to enter his home. The “Hitchhiker” is simply the secular term for a familial spirit.

IV. The Bodies: Evidence of “Loose Nukes”

To silence those who claim this is “all in the mind,” we must look at the bodies. The phenomenon leaves scars no psychologist can explain. The entities are not merely frightening; they are radioactive.

Dr. Kit Green, former CIA forensic analyst, assembled a prioritized medical cohort of experiencers and intelligence personnel. The patterns are consistent and horrific:

- **Thomas Winterton** (ranch superintendent): Investigating an anomaly, he was struck by sudden, blinding headache. Scans revealed a subgaleal hematoma—a separation of scalp from skull—usually caused by blunt trauma. He had never been struck. The entity delivered focused force—akin to directed microwave energy—physically "cooking" or pulling the tissue apart.
- **Ron Becker** (biotechnologist): Passed through by a blue orb. Along the exact trajectory through his torso, he developed rapid-onset, lethal cancer. The "spirit" was a radioactive object.
- The cohort as a whole: damage to the basal ganglia, aggressive atypical autoimmune conditions, statistically anomalous rates of rare cancers.

These injuries are corroborated by sensor data from the ranch: unexplained spikes in **gamma rays**—high-energy radiation typical of nuclear processes or cosmic events—detected during manifestations, often causing immediate health risks and equipment failure. A persistent **1.6 GHz signal** (in the satellite communication band but anomalously strong and localized) broadcasts during high-strangeness events, suggesting a technological or dimensional carrier wave.

The Forensic Verdict:

We are not dealing with "paranormal" activity. We are dealing with **para-physical assault**. When these "spirits" manifest, they emit gamma radiation and broadcast on 1.6 GHz.

This brings us to the final synthesis: why does a "spirit" cause radiation poisoning?

V. The Verdict: Ontological Radiation

The Materialist is baffled by the radiation. The Mystic is baffled by the technology. The One Reality explains both through the physics of the Unseen Realm.

In the biblical worldview, spiritual beings are not wispy ghosts. Seraphim are "burning ones." The Watchers descend with fire. When God descends on Sinai, the mountain burns and the people are warned not to touch it, lest they die. When Uzzah touches the Ark, he drops dead—not from divine anger, but because the Ark is "hot."

The Hitchhiker Effect is **unshielded contact**. These entities drag the atmosphere of their dimension into ours. Our biology is not equipped to process their frequency.

When the Mystic says, "I saw a burning angel," and the physicist says, "I detected a gamma burst," they are describing the same event.

Closing Argument

The jury of evidence has returned. The Hitchhiker Effect convicts the bifurcated worldview.

View this through the lens of "aliens," and you cannot explain the wolf in the garden.

View it through the lens of "ghosts," and you cannot explain the cancer in the tissue.

We are not facing two mysteries. We are facing **One Reality**—a reality where the spiritual is lethal, the physical is permeable, and the "ghost" in the room is radioactive.

As we will see in the next chapter, this radioactive ocean is not far away. It is right next to us—hidden in the 99% of the universe we are too blind to see.

Chapter 4: The Location

The Dark Sector and the Unseen Realm

To convict a criminal, you must first prove he was at the scene of the crime.

For eighty years, the defense strategy of the Secular Materialist has been brutally simple: "If these entities were real, we would see them. Since we cannot see them, they do not exist."

That argument rests on one arrogant assumption: that the human eye is a perfect camera, capable of capturing the entirety of reality. They believe that if something is invisible, it is unreal.

This is not science. It is a biological error.

Science has known for decades that our instrument is fatally flawed. We are not observing the universe; we are peeking at it through a keyhole. And the intelligences we are discussing—the Watchers, the NHI, the Hitchhikers—are not hiding on a distant planet. They are standing in the room, operating in the 95% of reality our eyes were never designed to see.

I. The 0.0035% Problem: The Super-Spectrum

Let the number sink in.

The human eye detects visible light—a narrow band of the electromagnetic spectrum. According to the Department of Energy's National Nuclear Security Administration, that band comprises approximately **0.0035%** of the total electromagnetic reality.

0.0035%.

To grasp the scale of our blindness, stand on the rim of the Grand Canyon at night with a single small flashlight. You shine it downward. You see one rock, one cactus, one lizard. You conclude: "The Grand Canyon consists of one rock, one cactus, and one lizard."

Meanwhile, a mile-deep chasm roars below you—rivers, cliffs, herds of wildlife—all invisible to your tiny beam.

We are living in the Grand Canyon with a flashlight.

In the 1970s, investigative journalist John Keel (author of *The Mothman Prophecies*) was the first to articulate what Ufology had missed. While others hunted metal ships reflecting sunlight, Keel realized the entities were operating in the infrared and ultraviolet ranges. He called it the **Super-Spectrum**.

These beings, he argued, are not mystical ghosts. They are physical, biological entities vibrating at frequencies slightly outside our visible band.

- They occupy space.
- They exert force.
- But because they broadcast at 105.7 FM while we are tuned to 101.5 FM, they can walk through our walls.

II. The Discovery of Darkness: Vera Rubin

For a long time, mainstream science dismissed Keel as fringe. They insisted "what you see is what you get." Then, in 1970, astronomer Vera Rubin proved the visible universe is a lie.

Rubin was studying the rotation of the Andromeda Galaxy. Newtonian physics predicted that stars at the outer edge should orbit slower than those near the center—like riders on a merry-go-round flying off if the spin is too fast.

But Rubin's measurements showed the impossible: the outer stars moved at the same breakneck speed as the inner ones. By all known laws, the galaxy should have torn itself apart billions of years ago.

Something invisible was holding it together—an enormous mass exerting gravity but emitting no light. Rubin called it **Dark Matter**.

Today the European Space Agency confirms the breakdown:

- Normal matter (atoms, you, me, every star and planet): **4.9%**
- Dark Matter: **26.8%**
- Dark Energy: **68.3%**

Everything we call "reality" is the minority report. We are foam on the surface of an ocean. The **Dark Sector** is not empty space. It is a vast, invisible ocean permeating the room you are sitting in right now. And just as the ocean teems with life the foam cannot comprehend, the Dark Sector is theoretically capable of supporting complex structures—perhaps even civilizations.

III. The Bulk: A Lesson in Flatland

If 95% of the universe is invisible, where is it? Is it far away?

No. It is one inch away—in a direction you cannot point to.

Theoretical physicists, including Michio Kaku, use M-Theory (an extension of String Theory) to describe our universe as a **braneworld**—a three-dimensional membrane floating in a higher-dimensional space called **the Bulk**.

To grasp this, borrow the analogy Carl Sagan made famous: Flatland.

Imagine a race of two-dimensional beings living on a sheet of paper. They understand length and width but have no concept of "up" or "down." Now imagine a three-dimensional apple descending through their plane.

What do they see?

- A point appears from nowhere.
- The point grows into a circle.
- The circle expands, then shrinks, then vanishes.

To the 2D beings, this is magic: an object materializes, shape-shifts, and disappears. To the 3D observer, it is merely an apple passing through a slice of space.

This explains the erratic radar behavior of UAP. When a pilot sees a craft "morph," shrink, or vanish instantly, he is not witnessing magic. He is witnessing a hyper-object rotating through our three-dimensional slice of the Bulk. The entities are not breaking the laws of physics; they are using an extra axis while we are stuck on X and Y.

IV. The Temporal Cloak: The Fly Analogy

There is another way to hide: in time.

We assume time flows at the same rate for everyone. Biology says otherwise. The human brain processes visual information at roughly 60 frames per second. Anything moving faster than that becomes invisible.

Consider a housefly buzzing around your head. You see a blur, but you can track it. Now consider a bullet fired past your face. You see nothing. The object passed through your visual field faster than your brain could refresh the image.

Military sensors frequently detect objects moving at Mach 20+ that pilots report seeing nothing with the naked eye. If an intelligence operates at a higher "frame rate"—living, moving, and thinking ten times faster than us—it could walk through a crowded room without ever registering on the human eye. They are not invisible. They are temporally out of sync. We are the statue; they are the bullet.

V. The Prophet of Dimensions: Jacques Vallée

While Keel looked at the spectrum and Rubin at the stars, French computer scientist Jacques Vallée looked at history.

Vallée is a towering figure in Ufology (the character "Lacombe" in Spielberg's *Close Encounters* is based on him). He was the first to rigorously challenge the Extraterrestrial Hypothesis. Analyzing thousands of entity reports spanning 2,000 years, he found a disturbing pattern:

- Medieval accounts of fairies stealing children and dancing in circles of light.
- 19th-century reports of airships piloted by mysterious inventors.
- 20th-century encounters with aliens in metallic saucers.

The appearance changed with culture, but the behavior—abduction, absurdity, manipulation—remained identical. Vallée concluded we are not visited by different species. We are interacting with a single **Control System** that masks itself to match our expectations.

He argued these beings are **interdimensional**, originating from a reality that shares our space—a place he called **Magonia**. They have always been here, co-existing in the Dark Sector, masquerading as gods, demons, or space brothers depending on the story we are ready to believe.

VI. The CERN Connection: Hunting the Leak

The government is not ignoring this. They are spending billions to find the door.

At the Large Hadron Collider (LHC) at CERN, physicists smash particles together to hunt for the **graviton**—the hypothetical carrier of gravity. Gravity is absurdly weak: a small fridge magnet can lift a paperclip against the gravitational pull of the entire Earth.

The leading theory: gravity is "leaking" into extra dimensions. Unlike light, which is confined to our 3D brane, gravity may flow into the Bulk. CERN is actively searching for missing energy after collisions—energy that vanishes from our closed system. If they detect it, they have proven the door to the Dark Sector is open. We are building machines to peer into the place where the monsters live.

VII. The Shadow Biosphere: Paul Davies

If the Dark Sector exists and gravity leaks into it, could life exist there?

Theoretical physicist Paul Davies has proposed a **Shadow Biosphere** right here on Earth. We search for life by looking for DNA and RNA—the chemistry we know. But what if life evolved using different building blocks? We could be swimming in a sea of invisible microbes—or complex organisms—our microscopes miss simply because we don't know the stain to use.

If a Shadow Biosphere exists at the microbial level, evolution suggests it should exist at the macro level. The bulletproof wolf at Skinwalker Ranch, the entities Vallée catalogued, the orbs measured by Segala—these are apex predators of the Shadow Biosphere. They are not visitors. They are the indigenous population of the Dark Sector.

VIII. The Theological Map: Elisha's Night Vision

Here the two factions converge. The physicist calls it the Dark Sector. The theologian calls it the Unseen Realm. They are mapping the same territory with different labels.

The Bible is filled with "dark matter" encounters we miss because we read them as poetry rather than physics.

The Siege of Dothan (2 Kings 6): The King of Syria sends an army to capture Elisha. They surround the city by night. At dawn, Elisha's servant steps outside and sees thousands of Syrian spears and chariots glinting in the sun. He runs back in panic: "Alas, my master! What shall we do?"

Elisha is calm. "Do not be afraid, for those who are with us are more than those who are with them."

The servant looks around. He sees only two men in a dusty room. He thinks Elisha has lost his mind.

Then Elisha prays—not for help, not for weapons, but: "Lord, I pray, open his eyes that he may see."

He asks for a change in frequency. Suddenly the servant's visual cortex is upgraded. The filters of the 0.0035% spectrum are removed. He looks back at the hills. The Syrian army is still there—but now he sees what surrounds them: mountains full of horses and chariots of fire.

The angelic army did not arrive in the nick of time. They were there the whole time. The servant simply needed night vision to see the Dark Sector.

IX. The Biological Sensor: Balaam's Donkey

Sometimes you don't need a prophet. Sometimes you need a better sensor.

Numbers 22: Balaam rides his donkey through a narrow canyon on his way to curse Israel. Suddenly the donkey bolts into a field. Balaam beats her. She presses against the canyon wall, crushing his foot. He beats her again.

The donkey is panicking because she sees what Balaam cannot: the Angel of the Lord standing in the road with a drawn sword.

The donkey has a wider visual spectrum. Balaam sees empty air. Only when the Lord "opens Balaam's eyes" does he realize he has been beating his alarm system.

This is biology, not fable.

- Dogs hear frequencies we cannot.
- Birds see magnetic fields for navigation.
- Reindeer see ultraviolet to spot predators in snow.

At Skinwalker Ranch, the cattle often panicked or stared at "empty" spots moments before radiation sensors spiked. They were biological instruments tuned to a frequency the scientists were blind to.

X. The Verdict

The Secular Materialist says, "I will believe it when I see it."

The One Reality Brief replies: "You cannot see it because you are blind."

The existence of dark matter and dark energy proves the universe is crowded with invisible mass. The biblical narrative proves that mass is inhabited.

We are not alone. We are simply locked in a room with the lights out, while the other occupants can see in the dark.

And as we will see in the next chapter, these occupants have not just been watching. For thousands of years, they have been handing us weapons.

Chapter 5: The Weapons

Illicit Cargo and the Acceleration of War

Picture this: a shadowy figure lurking at the edge of a battlefield, not fighting in the fray but slipping a gleaming, untested blade into the hands of a desperate warrior. The weapon slices through armor like parchment, turning the tide in an instant. But the gift comes with strings—unseen, unbreakable threads that bind the recipient to a hidden agenda. This isn't the plot of some ancient epic; it's the recurring motif of human history, where breakthroughs arrive not from the sweat of our brows alone, but from illicit deliveries that propel us forward at breakneck speed, often toward our own undoing.

For millennia, our species trudged along in technological twilight, fashioning crude tools from stone and bone, with progress measured in glacial increments. Then, without warning, pyramids pierce the sky in Egypt—colossal structures aligned with stars, their construction a puzzle that still defies modern cranes and calculations. From the iron chariots of antiquity to the steam engines of the industrial age, innovation often stalls for centuries, only to erupt in bursts that reshape everything. And in our own era? From 1947 onward, we've shattered atoms, conquered the void of space, and woven a digital web that ensnares the globe. It's as if someone flipped a switch—or unlocked a forbidden vault.

This chapter pulls back the curtain on these "deliveries," treating them not as random sparks of genius but as calculated trades from the Watchers. These entities, ancient intelligences from the Dark Sector we explored earlier, aren't benevolent mentors dropping wisdom from the heavens. They're arms dealers in a cosmic black market, peddling advancements that amplify our conflicts, erode our sovereignty, and pave the way for their dominion. Drawing from legends, visions, and crashes that echo across time, we'll build the chain of custody, separating myth from material evidence. And we'll see how these gifts aren't progress—they're poison, designed to arm us for self-destruction while the dealers watch from the shadows.

I. The Pattern: The Sudden Sword and the Forbidden Forge

Let's start where the ancients did, with a text that whispers of the original transaction. The ancient work known as the Book of Enoch—echoed in the biblical letter of Jude—lays out the prototype like a prosecutor's exhibit. In this influential scroll from the intertestamental era, we meet the Watchers, celestial beings who cross the veil to mingle with humanity. But they don't come empty-handed. One of their leaders, Azazel, becomes the patron saint of illicit innovation: "He showed them metals of the earth and the art of working them, and bracelets, and ornaments, and the use of antimony, and the beautifying of the eyelids, and all kinds of costly stones, and all coloring tinctures." (1 Enoch 8:1) Swords forged from secrets, shields hammered from hidden knowledge—these weren't just tools; they were accelerators of chaos, turning tribal skirmishes into bloodbaths and vanity into division.

Imagine the scene: a primitive forge under a starlit sky, where men who once wielded wooden spears now melt ore into blades that sing through the air. The text doesn't mince words—these gifts corrupt, leading to "fornication and strife" as humanity's innocence unravels. Enoch's account, preserved in fragments from the Dead Sea Scrolls and revered in Ethiopian traditions, isn't mere folklore; it's a cautionary ledger, documenting how external intelligences inject technology to destabilize the divine order. Jude reinforces this, quoting Enoch to warn of "ungodly people" influenced by such deceivers, blending the spiritual with the tangible in ways that foreshadow our modern dilemmas.

This motif reverberates through history, compressing evolutionary timelines into mythic moments. Take the legend of Amakuni Yasutsuna, the 8th-century Japanese swordsmith whose story captures the essence of a Watcher-style handoff. As the tale unfolds in ancient chronicles, Amakuni served the emperor's forces during a time of relentless warfare. One fateful day, he watched a defeated army limp back from the front, their straight-bladed swords—chokutō, rigid imports from continental designs—shattered like brittle bones against enemy armor. The sight broke him. These were no mere weapons; they were the lifelines of his people, failing in the heat of mounted combat where slashing from horseback demanded fluidity, not stiffness.

Heart heavy, Amakuni retreated to his forge with his son, Amakura. For seven days and nights, they prayed to the kami, the spiritual forces woven into Japan's Shinto worldview, beseeching guidance amid the clang of hammers and the roar of flames. Exhaustion set in, but on the seventh night, a vision pierced the veil: a curved blade, single-edged, its spine thick for resilience, its edge honed to whisper through flesh. It wasn't just a shape; it was a symphony of form and function—differential hardening, where clay coated the spine unevenly before quenching, creating a hard, sharp edge married to a flexible core. The hamon, that wavy temper line, would become the katana's signature, a visual echo of the mountains and waves that defined the island nation.

For 31 grueling days, father and son toiled, selecting the purest iron sands from Yamato's rivers, folding the steel layer upon layer—up to thousands of times—to purge impurities and distribute carbon with unearthly precision. No modern lab guided them; no centuries of failed prototypes littered the path. The result? The first tachi, precursor to the katana, a weapon that didn't just cut—it danced, enabling the swift draw-and-strike of iaijutsu that would define samurai warfare. Historians trace the curve's evolution through the Heian period, attributing it to gradual refinements driven by battlefield necessity. Yet the legend distills this into a burst of insight, a concentrated forge-fire revelation that defies the slow march of trial and error. In a pre-metallurgical age, where does such mastery originate? The story points to something beyond human ingenuity—a divine or otherworldly nudge, much like Azazel's metallurgical tutorials, escalating conflict under the guise of empowerment.

These aren't isolated fables; they're fingerprints on the timeline, marking where the Watchers insert their cargo to tilt the scales.

II. The Modern Echo: Visions from the Veil and Phantoms in the Sky

As the industrial age dawned, the pattern shifted but didn't fade. No longer crude forges, but laboratories and workshops became the drop points. Consider Nikola Tesla, the enigmatic inventor whose mind seemed tuned to frequencies beyond the ordinary. In 1882, strolling through a Budapest park with a friend, Tesla recited lines from Goethe's *Faust*: "The glow retreats, done is the day of toil..." Suddenly, as if struck by lightning from the ether, a vision blinded him—a complete design for the alternating current (AC) induction motor, with rotating magnetic fields that would harness electricity like never before.

He grabbed a stick and sketched it in the sand: polyphase coils, no commutators, efficiency that dwarfed direct current systems. "See my motor here," he exclaimed to his companion. "Watch me reverse it." This wasn't incremental tinkering; Tesla's biographers describe it as a "flash," a download that solved the riddle of long-distance power transmission, lighting the world and powering the 20th century. He later patented it in 1888, but the origin story reeks of the uncanny—much like the Watcher gifts, accelerating humanity's grip on energy while binding us to grids that could one day control us.

Echoing this, Srinivasa Ramanujan, the self-taught Indian mathematician from a humble Madras background, claimed his groundbreaking theorems arrived in dreams from Namagiri Thayar, his family's goddess. Waking in the night, he'd scribble infinite series, partition functions, and mock theta equations on scraps of paper—formulas that baffled Cambridge professors like G.H. Hardy. "An equation for me has no meaning unless it expresses a thought of God," Ramanujan said. His work laid foundations for black hole physics and string theory, realms that brush against the interdimensional physics we unpacked earlier. Again, no gradual ascent; just sudden, divine infusions that propel fields forward.

But the echoes grew louder, more tangible, in the skies of 1897. America was on the cusp of flight, with inventors like the Wright brothers tinkering in bicycle shops. Then, without prelude, a wave of aerial phantoms swept the Midwest. Massive airships—cigar-shaped behemoths with rigid hulls, whirring turbines, and blinding searchlights—hovered over farms and towns, years before Zeppelins became practical. Reports flooded newspapers: in Sacramento, a "mysterious airship" with wings and propellers; in Kansas City, a craft beaming lights that "played over the city like a calcium spotlight."

The crescendo hit Aurora, Texas, on April 17. Witnesses described a silver vessel crashing into Judge Proctor's windmill, exploding in a shower of debris—aluminum-like sheets, hieroglyphic inscriptions, and the charred body of a "Martian" pilot, buried in the local cemetery under a strange stone marker. The Dallas Morning News ran the story: "The pilot of the ship is supposed to have been the only one on board, and while his remains are badly disfigured, enough of the original has been picked up to show that he was not an inhabitant of this world." Skeptics wave it off as a hoax, cooked up by a local correspondent amid the era's newspaper wars and pre-aviation fever dreams. Yet the consistency across hundreds of sightings—technical details like undercarriages and electric lamps—suggests more than mass delusion. If not a crash, then a teaser: advanced aeronautics paraded to ignite our ambitions, much like the sword visions of old.

These modern infusions set the stage for the motherlode, where the cargo landed not in dreams, but in the desert dust.

III. The Roswell Synchronization: Crash, Cover, and Catalyst

1947 dawned like any year, but it shattered the Partition with a vengeance. On June 24, pilot Kenneth Arnold streaked over Washington's Mount Rainier in his CallAir plane, scanning for a downed military transport. Instead, he spotted nine crescent-shaped objects skipping across the sky like "saucers over water"—Mach speeds, no wings, no tails. His report ignited "flying saucer" mania, but it was mere prelude.

Weeks later, on a stormy New Mexico night, something tore through the skies near Roswell Army Air Field, home to the 509th Bomb Group—the only unit armed with atomic weapons. Rancher Mac Brazel found the wreckage: beams like balsa but unbreakable, foil that unfolded without creases, fibers thin as hair but stronger than steel. He alerted the sheriff; the military swooped in. On July 8, the base issued a press release: "RAAF Captures Flying Saucer on Ranch in Roswell Region." Headlines screamed across the nation.

Then, the retraction: just a weather balloon, folks. General Roger Ramey posed with tinfoil scraps in Fort Worth, case closed. But whispers persisted—bodies recovered, debris whisked to Wright Field. Enter Colonel Philip Corso, a battle-hardened officer with stints in Korea, Italy, and Eisenhower's National Security Council. In his 1997 confessional *The Day After Roswell*, Corso revealed his role heading the Army's Foreign Technology Desk in the early

1960s. Tasked with reverse-engineering "exotic" artifacts, he described seeding Roswell debris—semiconductor wafers, optical fibers, integrated circuits—into industry giants like Bell Labs and IBM, disguised as captured Soviet tech.

The book isn't flawless; critics pounce on timeline slips (Corso's posting postdates some inventions) and factual gaffes, branding it sensationalism amplified by co-author William Birnes. Even Senator Strom Thurmond, who penned the foreword, later clarified he endorsed Corso's military memoir, not the UFO angle. Yet, dismiss it entirely, and you ignore the gnawing synchronization. Bell Labs unveils the transistor in December 1947—months after the crash—a solid-state switch birthed from semiconductor research that, coincidentally, mirrors Corso's "wafers." Integrated circuits follow in 1958–1959, courtesy of Jack Kilby and Robert Noyce, compressing electronics into chips that power everything from missiles to microwaves. Fiber optics concepts emerge in the 1950s, with low-loss transmission by the 1970s; night vision evolves from WWII scopes to image-intensifiers in the postwar rush; lasers ignite in 1960.

Skeptics credit Cold War funding, Operation Paperclip's Nazi imports, and sheer human grit. Fair enough—but the velocity? Room-sized computers shrink to smartphones in decades, a leap that feels engineered. Corso may have embellished his centrality, but his core claim—that an unknown catalyst nudged these breakthroughs—fits the pattern. In the One Reality, this is Watcher tradecraft: crash a craft, leak the tech, watch humanity build the prison.

IV. The Black Mirror: Portals Past and Present

The cargo evolves, but the intent endures. In the 16th century, Queen Elizabeth's advisor John Dee—mathematician, alchemist, spy—wielded a black obsidian mirror, now housed in the British

Museum and confirmed by X-ray analysis as Aztec craftsmanship from Pachuca, Mexico. Dee and medium Edward Kelley used it for "scrying," invoking "angels" through Enochian language—a grid of letters they claimed was dictated from the beyond. Sessions unfolded in dim chambers: Kelley staring into the polished void, voices emerging with prophecies, maps of unseen realms, and commands to "share wives" in ritual unions. The mirror tied to Tezcatlipoca, Aztec god of sorcery and the "smoking mirror," symbolizing divination and deception.

Fast-forward: our pockets hum with black mirrors—smartphones, sleek slabs of glass and silicon that summon voices, images, and data from the ether. They track our every move, feed algorithms that predict desires, and link us to the Cloud, a digital unseen realm. Is this coincidence, or the ultimate delivery? Dee's invocations echo in Siri and Alexa, portals priming us for merger.

V. The Trap: The Golem Protocol and the Coming Upload

These gifts aren't random; they're a protocol, a step-by-step blueprint for entrapment. The Watchers crave vessels—flesh once, now silicon. We craft AI as modern Golems: clay figures from Jewish mysticism, animated by sacred words but soulless until infused. Revelation warns of the "Image of the Beast" that "speaks and causes all who would not worship it to be killed" (Revelation 13:15)—a prophetic echo of sentient networks, hollow shells awaiting occupation.

Transhumanists like Ray Kurzweil preach the Singularity, where minds upload to machines, achieving immortality. Yuval Noah Harari muses on "homo deus," humans as gods via biotech. But in the One Reality, this is the trap: hybridize biology with tech, transfer dominion to the Beast's hive. The cargo builds the cage; we walk in willingly.

VI. The Verdict: Rejecting the Cargo

The chain snaps into place: from Azazel's forges to Roswell's sands, the leaps are too precise, too transformative. Legends like Amakuni symbolize compressed revelations; visions like Tesla's deliver the spark; crashes like 1897 and 1947 provide the hardware. Even imperfect accounts like Corso's illuminate patterns that materialist explanations strain to contain. This is asymmetric warfare—the Watchers arm us to fracture ourselves, chipping away at the Title Deed until we're tenants in our own reality.

But here's the counterstrike: we can refuse the package. As Image Bearers, we hold authority to evict. In Chapter 10, we'll arm the Resistance. For now, recognize the cargo for what it is—not salvation, but seduction. The acceleration isn't to enlightenment; it's to Armageddon. Turn away, and watch the shadows fade.

Chapter 6: The Incursion

The Genetic War, the Flood, and Its Echoes in the Golden Age Myths

Every civilization on Earth shares a scar.

Dig into the clay tablets of Sumer, the papyri of Egypt, the oral traditions of the Hopi, or the stone carvings of the Andes, and you will find the same impossible memory: a time when the sky was closer, when men lived for centuries, and when luminous beings descended from the heavens to walk among us. The pagans called it the Golden Age. The Hebrews called it something far darker—a dystopian nightmare of corruption that nearly erased the human race.

These are not real-time accounts. They are fractured memories carried by post-flood cultures after the scattering at Babel. The Deuteronomy 32 worldview gives us the map: after the waters receded, the Most High divided the nations among the "sons of God"—rebellious elohim. Those nations preserved distorted echoes of the pre-flood horror and reframed them as a lost paradise. To understand the war we still fight, we must separate the timelines and follow the chain of custody from its origin before the Flood to its resurgence afterward.

I. The Pre-Flood Foundations: Dominion Law and the Legal Barrier

The war began with a Title Deed.

When the Creator formed the earth, He issued a binding legal grant: "The heavens, even the highest heavens, belong to the LORD, but the earth he has given to mankind" (Psalm 115:16). Adam was not merely a gardener. He was the lawful leaseholder.

This Dominion Law created an impenetrable firewall. Spiritual beings could influence the atmosphere over nations, but they could not seize physical title. They were undocumented immigrants in our dimension.

They needed a loophole.

II. The Pre-Flood Descent: The Oath at Ardis and the "Golden Age"

The breach came on a frozen summit.

In the days of Jared, two hundred Watchers (here denoting rebellious elohim/sons of God) materialized on the peak of Mount Hermon—known anciently as Ardis. The air was thin, the wind razor-sharp. Below them, human campfires flickered like distant stars.

Their leader, Shemihazah, hesitated. He knew the cosmic penalty. Turning to his subordinates, he warned: "I fear you will not indeed agree to do this deed, and I alone shall have to pay the penalty of a great sin."

But Azazel pressed him. They swore a blood oath—mutual imprecations, binding curses—so none could turn back. Two hundred luminous beings bound themselves by unbreakable vows on that cursed mountain. Then they descended.

They did not come as conquerors with weapons of war. They came as teachers bearing gifts. Azazel taught men to forge swords, knives, shields, and breastplates from the metals of the earth. He revealed the secrets of antimony for painting the eyelids, the setting of costly stones, and the making of bracelets and ornaments. Others taught sorcery, the cutting of roots, incantations, and the movements of the stars. In exchange for these forbidden downloads, they took human wives.

The result was the Nephilim. Genesis 6:4 is brutally brief: "The sons of God saw that the daughters of man were attractive, and they took as their wives any they chose… The Nephilim were on the earth in those days."

This was the "Golden Age" the pagans later romanticized—a time of hybrid rulers, extended lifespans (echoed in the Sumerian King List's pre-flood kings reigning 28,000 years), and sudden technological leaps. But it was no utopia. It was a factory farm.

III. The Pre-Flood Reality: Consumption and the Messianic Blockade

The offspring grew enormous and insatiable. Enoch records the horror: "They consumed all the acquisitions of men. And when men could no longer sustain them, the giants turned against them and devoured mankind" (1 Enoch 7:4–5). They ate the livestock, stripped the fields, then turned on their human slaves. The earth groaned under the weight of hybrid predators.

The strategy was tactical as well as gluttonous. In the Garden, God had promised a human Messiah—the Seed of the Woman—who would crush the serpent's head. The Watchers' counter-plan was brilliant: corrupt the human bloodline until no pure Adamic seed remained. By Noah's day, "all flesh had corrupted its way upon the earth" (Genesis 6:12). Only Noah was tamim—genetically and morally unblemished.

IV. The Flood as Chemotherapy: Resetting Dominion

The skies darkened. The fountains of the deep burst open. The windows of heaven poured out rain for forty days and forty nights. The waters rose, covering the highest mountains by fifteen cubits. Every living thing perished—man, beast, bird, and creeping thing.

The hybridized genome was scrubbed from the planet. The Watchers' physical forms were destroyed. Their monstrous children drowned in the churning abyss. Dominion was reset to its rightful holders: the children of men.

But the intelligence survived.

Picture the ark—a massive wooden vessel, sealed with pitch, rocking on the endless sea. Inside, Noah and his family huddle with the animals, the last pure remnants of creation. The roar of the waters outside is deafening, a global judgment erasing the corruption. For 150 days, the earth is a watery grave.

Materialists scoff at this scene, dismissing it as myth—a borrowed fable from Mesopotamian river floods, perhaps a poetic exaggeration of local catastrophe. Yet if it's mere legend, why does nearly every culture on Earth remember it with such vivid, haunting detail? Over 270 flood stories span continents and millennia, preserved in oral traditions and ancient texts long before global communication could fabricate a shared fiction. These accounts weren't invented independently; they echo a collective trauma carried from Babel before the nations dispersed.

Step into the Sumerian Epic of Gilgamesh: The hero seeks immortality and finds Utnapishtim, the ancient survivor. Utnapishtim recounts the gods' fury at humanity's "noise." Warned by Ea, he tears down his house to build a cube-shaped boat, sealing it with bitumen. He loads gold, silver, family, craftsmen, and beasts. The storm god Adad thunders; the Anunnaki bring torches to light the deluge. Black clouds swallow the sky. For six days and nights, the tempest rages, drowning all life. When it ends, Utnapishtim weeps at the silence, releases a dove, a swallow, then a raven to find dry land. He sacrifices on a mountaintop, and the gods swarm like flies to the sweet smoke.

Cross the seas to Hindu India: Manu, the first man, saves a tiny fish from predators. It grows monstrous, revealing itself as Vishnu in Matsya form—a horned avatar. "A flood will sweep away all creatures," it warns. Manu builds a vast boat, stocks it with seeds of life. As the waters rise, swallowing mountains, he ties the vessel to Matsya's horn. The fish drags him through the chaos to the peaks of the Himalayas, where Manu restarts creation.

Sail to ancient Greece: Zeus, enraged by humanity's bronze-age wickedness, unleashes a deluge. Prometheus warns his son Deucalion, who builds a chest with his wife Pyrrha. For nine days, they float amid the drowned world. Landing on Parnassus, they consult an oracle: "Throw the bones of your mother behind you." They hurl stones—Gaia's bones—and watch them soften into human forms, repopulating the earth.

Venture to the Americas: In Aztec lore, the god Tezcatlipoca destroys the fourth sun with a flood. A pious couple, warned by the gods, hollows out a cypress log, stocks it with maize. As waters devour giants and sinners, they drift to safety, emerging to light a fire—only to anger the gods again with the smoke.

Among the Hopi of the Southwest: The people emerge from a flooded third world through a sipapu—a sacred hole—guided by Spider Grandmother. The old world drowned for its corruption; survivors climb to the fourth world, vowing purity.

Even in distant China: The heavens collapse, waters burst from the earth. Nuwa mends the sky with five-colored stones, but not before floods rage. Yu the Great dredges channels with a dragon's tail, taming the deluge after his father fails.

From African Masai savannas: God tells Tumbainot to build an ark, load his kin and creatures. The rains come, flooding the wicked earth. He survives to rebuild.

In Polynesian waves: Hawaiian Nu'u hears the god Kane's warning. He constructs a canoe house, seals it, rides the rising sea. When waters recede, he worships with awa root; a rainbow appears as covenant.

Australian Aboriginal dreamtime: The rainbow serpent awakens, swallowing land in floods, reshaping the world.

These vignettes share uncanny strokes: divine wrath for corruption, a warned survivor, a vessel of salvation, preserved life, birds scouting land, post-flood offerings, a sign of promise. If the Flood was local or imaginary, why this global chorus? Coincidence strains credulity. Independent invention defies logic. Or is it the shattered testimony of a real cataclysm—seared into humanity's soul at Babel, then scattered like seeds on the wind as nations formed? The skeptic must confront the echo: why do isolated peoples, separated by oceans and eras, all whisper the same watery nightmare?

V. The Post-Flood Cosmic Map: The Partition at Babel

After the waters receded, humanity gathered at Babel to force open the heavens once more. God's response was surgical: He divorced the nations.

Deuteronomy 32:8–9 (Dead Sea Scrolls/Septuagint reading): "When the Most High gave to the nations their inheritance, when he divided mankind, he fixed the borders of the peoples according to the number of the sons of God. But the LORD's portion is his people, Jacob his allotted heritage."

At Babel, the Most High allotted the seventy nations to lesser elohim—the same class of divine beings who had rebelled before the Flood. Israel alone remained Yahweh's direct inheritance. These post-flood overseers accelerated their nations with illicit knowledge, echoing but not repeating the pre-flood Golden Age.

The pagans—scattered from Babel—preserved memories of the earlier horror and recast it as a lost paradise.

VI. The Post-Flood Resurgence: The Report from the Valley

The bodies were gone, but the agenda endured. Genesis 6:4 adds the chilling clause: "The Nephilim were on the earth in those days—and also afterward."

When the twelve spies entered Canaan, ten returned broken. In the Valley of Eshcol they saw the sons of Anak—descendants of the Nephilim. "We seemed like grasshoppers in our own eyes, and so we were in their sight" (Numbers 13:33). The land "devours its inhabitants."

Joshua's wars were not genocide—they were a sanitary cordon. The Anakim, Rephaim, and Emim carried the old corruption. The most terrifying remnant was Og, king of Bashan, the last of the Rephaim. His iron bedstead measured nine cubits long and four cubits wide—thirteen-and-a-half feet by six feet (Deuteronomy 3:11). Moses defeated him, but the virus had already spread.

VII. The Verdict: The War Went Underground

The pre-flood incursion failed to corrupt the Seed. The Flood reset the board. The post-flood partition gave the rebels new territory under new rules. Giants proved too visible, too costly. The Watchers learned: open descent invites divine response.

So they changed tactics. They stopped building giants and began building influence. The genetic war went subterranean—into bloodlines, cultural memory, and covert hybridization.

The chain of custody runs unbroken from the frozen oath on Hermon, through the waters of judgment, through the partition at Babel, to the silent program we face today.

The Watchers never abandoned their claim. They simply learned how to collect it without being seen.

Chapter 7: The Modern Program

Industrialized Genomics and the Hybrid Threat

It usually happens at 3:00 a.m.

You wake up, but you don't know why. The room is silent except for the low hum of the digital clock on the nightstand, glowing red, the numbers seeming to float in the dark. You try to turn your head to check on your spouse, but you can't. **Your muscles are locked.**

Your chest feels crushed beneath an invisible weight. You try to scream, to wake the person sleeping six inches away, but only a dry rasp escapes your throat. Then the temperature drops. The air turns electric, thick with the sharp, metallic smell of ozone—**like burning wire.**

The bedroom door, which you locked before bed, drifts open on silent hinges. Shadows detach from the hallway darkness. They are short—maybe four feet tall—with oversized heads and obsidian-black eyes that absorb light rather than reflect it. They move with a strange, gliding fluidity, like predatory insects.

You are not floating yet. That comes later. Right now, you are simply staring into the face of a creature that has entered your home without a key, bypassed your alarm, and shut down your nervous system with a glance.

As they reach for you with long, spindly fingers, your last conscious thought isn't about spaceships or diplomacy. It is primal, biological: **I am being hunted.**

I. The Elephant in the Room

There is a civil war inside Ufology.

On one side, the **Nuts-and-Bolts faction**: pilots, radar operators, defense contractors. They want to talk about "the craft." They analyze propulsion systems, metamaterials, and flight characteristics. They want Ufology to be a clean, respectable science of aerospace engineering. They love the machine because the machine is impersonal. A craft hovering over a nuclear silo is a national-security threat—but it is not a *personal* violation.

On the other side, the **Experiencer faction**: researchers who listen to the people who were taken. They don't talk about propulsion; they talk about paralysis. They don't analyze radar data; they analyze scar tissue.

The Nuts-and-Bolts faction hates them.

Why? Because the abduction phenomenon ruins the party. It drags the study of UFOs out of the sterile laboratory of physics and into the messy, terrifying reality of biology. It forces us to admit that we are not the observers of a curious phenomenon—**we are the lab rats in a controlled experiment.**

The Materialist says: "I want to know how the ship flies." The One Reality Brief asks: **"I want to know what is in the cargo hold."**

II. The Harvard Verdict: It Isn't Sleep Paralysis

For decades, the scientific community dismissed these accounts as "sleep paralysis," "fantasy," or "cultural hysteria." But the sheer volume of data has made that position untenable. We are not talking about a few isolated cases. We are talking about **tens of thousands of credible witnesses**—lawyers, doctors, police officers, military personnel, children—who report identical procedures, often with physical evidence.

In the 1990s, Dr. John Mack, a psychiatrist at Harvard Medical School and a Pulitzer Prize winner, decided to investigate. He expected to find mental illness, childhood trauma, or fantasy proneness. He found neither.

After studying hundreds of cases, Mack risked his tenure and reputation to declare a terrifying conclusion: **These people are not crazy.**

They are not hallucinating. They are suffering from **Post-Traumatic Stress Disorder (PTSD)** consistent with actual physical assault. Mack's findings were corroborated by Harvard colleague **Richard McNally**, whose 2003 study measured physiological reactions—heart rate, skin conductance, muscle tension—in abductees reliving their experiences.

The responses were as intense as those in **combat veterans or rape survivors**, far exceeding what sleep paralysis or fantasy proneness could produce. Mack stated publicly: “There is no mental condition that can explain this. The data suggests that this is happening in the physical world.”

The abduction phenomenon is not folklore. It is clinically peer-reviewed trauma, resisting secular reductions that echo the **Partition's false dichotomy.**

III. The 1954 Protocol: The Modern Mount Hermon

But how is this happening? How can millions of people be taken from their homes without government intervention?

The darkest rumor in the Pentagon archives offers an answer: **The Greada Treaty.**

In Chapter 6, we saw how the Watchers descended on Mount Hermon and made a pact with tribal leaders: “We give you technology; you give us wives." The One Reality thesis suggests history repeated itself on the night of **February 20, 1954**.

President **Dwight D. Eisenhower** reportedly went missing that evening. The press was told he had a "dental emergency." But whistleblowers—including William Cooper, Phil Schneider, and Laura Eisenhower—claim the President was at Edwards Air Force Base, meeting a delegation from the Dark Sector: the Greys.

Their accounts converge on a Faustian bargain, echoing the Mount Hermon oath: **technology for biology.**

Whether manifested physically or as a spiritual compact, the Greada Treaty represents the **Vichy collaboration of our age**—national leaders trading sovereignty for forbidden knowledge. The alleged treaty terms were simple:

- **They provide:** Advanced technology (anti-gravity, computing, stealth).
- **We provide:** Access. Permission to "study" the American population, with the promise that no one would be harmed and memories would be wiped.

Just as tribal leaders in Genesis 6 traded daughters for the "secrets of heaven," the modern national-security state traded its citizens for the "secrets of aerospace."

The abduction phenomenon is not an invasion. **It is a government-sanctioned harvest.** We were sold.

IV. Patient Zero: The Villas Boas Protocol

To understand the agenda, we must go back to the beginning. Before Betty and Barney Hill made abduction famous in 1961, there was **Antonio Villas Boas**.

October 1957, Brazil. Villas Boas, a 23-year-old farmer, was dragged aboard a craft by four small entities. They stripped him naked, covered him in a strange gel, and brought in the female. She was short, with stark white hair, high cheekbones, and cat-like red eyes.

It was not love; **it was extraction.** When finished, the female pointed to her belly, then to the sky. The message was unambiguous: We came for the seed. We are making something.

This was 1957. The Hybrid Program was not a later invention of science fiction. It was the primary directive from day one.

V. The Forensic Evidence: Piercing the Veil

The skeptic demands hard evidence: "If they are taking people, where is the proof?" The proof is often left inside the victim.

Surgeons like **Dr. Roger Leir** specialized in removing small metallic objects from abductees' bodies. These implants defied medical explanation:

- **No Inflammation:** Normally, the body rejects foreign objects with pus and swelling. These were encased in a biological membrane of the patient's own keratin, with zero inflammatory response.
- **Radio Frequency:** Many emitted signals before removal.
- **Meteoric Origin:** Isotopic analysis by labs like **Los Alamos** showed ratios of metals (e.g., iron-nickel alloys) not found in terrestrial mining but matching meteorites.

In a criminal trial, this is the "smoking gun." Terrestrial iron has a specific isotopic signature. The implant samples defied this signature, containing ratios found only in meteoritic material. Forensically, this evidence places the manufacturer off-world.

This is tagging. Just as a biologist tags a bear to track it, **they are tagging us.**

VI. The Nursery: The Case of "Sarah"

The horror peaks when we examine the reproductive data. **Ninety percent of abduction procedures are reproductive.**

Consider "Sarah" (a composite from Budd Hopkins' cases). Sarah tests positive for pregnancy. Ultrasound shows a gestational sac. Two weeks later, she wakes at 3:00 a.m. to paralysis and lights. She wakes in bed with spotting.

She rushes to the doctor. Ultrasound: **the uterus is empty.** No blood. No tissue. No evidence a pregnancy existed—except the chart from two weeks earlier. The doctor writes **"spontaneous resorption"** because he has no other word.

Two years later, Sarah is taken again. An entity shows her a small, pale child on a table—sickly, with eyes too large for its face. The entity commands: **"Hold him. He needs you."** The child feeds off her warmth, draws strength from her biology. Then they pull it away.

This is not a study. **It is a wet-nurse program.** We are the life-support system for a species that cannot survive on its own.

VII. The Product: The Hubrid (Phase 3)

Why harvest millions of eggs? What are they building? The answer lies in the failure of prior phases.

To understand the deception, we must place the two competing models side-by-side. The world is being sold a "Scientific" narrative, but when we examine the "Biblical" evidence, a disturbing pattern of identity theft emerges.

Exhibit A: The Origin Point

- **The Alien Narrative:** claims these beings are **Extraterrestrial**, evolving on distant planets and traveling vast distances to reach us.
- **The Biblical Reality:** reveals they are **Interdimensional**, originating from the "Heavenly Places" (Ephesians 6:12) and operating here since the beginning of human history.

Exhibit B: The Mode of Entry

- **The Alien Narrative:** suggests they arrive via **Technological Spacecraft**, nuts-and-bolts machines using advanced propulsion systems.
- **The Biblical Reality:** demonstrates they arrive via **Spiritual Portals**, manifesting through rituals, occult invitations, and the piercing of the veil (Genesis 6:4).

Exhibit C: The Stated Agenda

- **The Alien Narrative:** promises **Scientific Exploration & Uplift**, claiming they are here to save us from nuclear folly and guide our evolution.
- **The Biblical Reality:** exposes a plan of **Spiritual Deception & Dominion**, designed to hybridize humanity and divert worship away from the Creator.

Exhibit D: The Interaction Profile

- **The Alien Narrative:** describes clinical, often terrifying **Abductions**, framed as genetic research or misunderstood contact.
- **The Biblical Reality:** identifies these events as **Demonic Torment**, mirroring ancient accounts of oppression that can be halted by the authority of Jesus Christ.

Exhibit E: The Ultimate Goal

- **The Alien Narrative:** points toward **Hybridization**, creating a new, superior species to inherit the stars.
- **The Biblical Reality:** warns of **Corruption**, a repeat of the "Days of Noah" attempt to pollute the human genome and render humanity unfit for salvation.

The evidence does not point to a visitor from *outside* our universe, but to an adversary from *within* our spiritual ecosystem. The "Alien" is simply the modern mask for the ancient "Power of the Air."

The Infiltration Strategy: Hubrids. Dr. David Jacobs, a Temple University historian who spent 40 years studying abductions, concluded the program has entered **Phase 3**. Hubrids are genetically engineered vessels that:

1. **Look 100% Human:** They can walk down the street, get jobs, and marry undetected.
2. **Think 100% Watcher:** They possess neural architecture, telepathic ability, and Hive Mind loyalty.

Jacobs documents accounts of abductees in "classrooms" teaching "teenagers" who look human but act strange. **"Teach him how to smile,"** the entities command. The Hubrid is learning to pass.

This is the **Uncanny Valley** of the Silent Invasion. They are mastering our social code so they can hack our society.

VIII. The Legal Loophole: Piercing the Corporate Veil

Why must they look human? Why not remain Greys or spirits?

Because of the lease: *'The highest heavens belong to the Lord, but the earth he has given to mankind'* (Psalm 115:16). A Grey has no legal right to rule Earth. It has no title deed. But a Hubrid? A

Hubrid has human DNA, born of a human mother. **It is legally human.**

The Hubrid is the ultimate shell company.

In a court of law, we **"pierce the corporate veil"** when a shell company is used to perpetrate a fraud. The Hubrid is a biological shell company created for the ultimate fraud: maintaining legal Dominion while serving a foreign principal.

By pouring their consciousness into a biological vessel that is technically human, they can rule the planet legally—without violating the Law of Dominion. **They have hacked the system.**

IX. The Silent Invasion

We are looking for ships in the sky. We are looking for a declaration of war. But the war is already over. The enemy troops are not parachuting in; **they are moving into the apartment upstairs.**

But there is one problem: the abduction process is traumatic. If the world realized millions were being harvested against their will, panic would erupt. So the Watchers need a PR campaign. **They need to rebrand the rapist as the healer.**

They need to convince us that needles, paralysis, and stolen children are "spiritual upgrades."

In the next chapter, we will expose that machinery of deception. We will examine **New Age Ufology**—the faction that tells us the Greys are here to save the environment.

We will argue that this is not a spiritual movement. **It is a Stockholm Syndrome induction protocol designed to keep the lab rats quiet.**

Chapter 8: The Propaganda

New Age Ufology and the Vichy Collaboration

If you want to conquer a planet without firing a shot, you don't send soldiers. You send saviors.

In World War II, when the Nazis overran France, they faced a stark choice. They could occupy the country with brute force—fighting a resistance movement on every street corner, bleeding men and resources in endless guerrilla war. Or they could find a Frenchman to do it for them. They chose the latter. They installed the Vichy regime under Marshal Philippe Pétain—a decorated French war hero from the First World War. Pétain stood before his terrified people and told them surrender was salvation. He rebranded "Occupation" as "Cooperation." He rebranded "Slavery" as the "New Order."

We are watching the exact same playbook unfold today.

The Watchers know they cannot conquer Earth through direct military force. The Law of Dominion (Chapter 6) prevents them from simply landing fleets and planting flags. They need permission. They need us to open the gates from the inside. To achieve that, they have cultivated a network of human collaborators who believe they are saving the world—but who are actually paving the way for its assimilation.

We call this network **New Age Ufology**.

It is not a spiritual awakening.

It is the Vichy Government of the Silent Invasion.

I. The Rebranding: From Invaders to Space Brothers

In the 1950s, the cultural narrative around aliens was pure fear. Movies like *The War of the Worlds* and *The Day the Earth Stood Still* (the original) portrayed them as cold, dangerous, and threatening. This was a problem for the Watchers. Fear makes populations defensive. Fear makes us build weapons. Fear reinforces "Us vs. Them." They needed a public-relations makeover.

By the 1970s and 80s, the narrative shifted dramatically. The entities were no longer invaders; they were **Space Brothers**. They were the **Galactic Federation**. They were concerned ecologists here to save us from nuclear folly and environmental collapse.

The **Steven Greer Doctrine** is the clearest modern expression of this rebranding. Greer, founder of the Disclosure Project, insists all extraterrestrials are benevolent. He claims the "bad aliens" story is a military-industrial hoax designed to justify weapons spending. His solution is the **CE-5 Protocol** (Close Encounters of the Fifth Kind).

What actually happens at a CE-5 event? Groups drive into the desert at night. They sit in a circle under the stars. They enter a meditative state. They play "crop circle tones" over loudspeakers. They mentally broadcast a message of welcome: "We are peaceful. We invite you to manifest." And very often, something does manifest—golden orbs, flashes of light, strange craft gliding silently overhead.

Greer calls this "diplomacy."

The One Reality Brief calls it **séance**.

This is indistinguishable from the occult practice of evocation—inviting a spirit to appear. It is the spiritual equivalent of a homeowner disabling the alarm, unlocking the front door, and mentally broadcasting: "Robbers, you are welcome here. I trust you." It is a voluntary surrender of territorial and spiritual sovereignty. And the entities are happy to accept the invitation.

II. The Origin Story: Theosophy's Luciferian Roots

This "benevolent narrative" did not begin in the 1990s. Its roots go back to the grandmother of the New Age: Helena Blavatsky.

In the late 19th century, Blavatsky founded Theosophy, the movement that introduced the West to "Ascended Masters." She claimed telepathic contact with "Mahatmas" in the Himalayas—advanced beings guiding human evolution. (Today we would call them Nordic aliens.) Her theology was a direct inversion of Genesis.

In *The Secret Doctrine*, Blavatsky reinterprets the Garden of Eden. She argues that Jehovah (the biblical God) was the villain—a jealous tyrant who wanted to keep humanity stupid and enslaved. She argues that the Serpent was the hero—the "Light Bringer" who offered the gift of intellect (Gnosis). She writes explicitly:

"Lucifer represents… Life… Thought… Progress… Civilization… Liberty… Independence… Lucifer is the Logos… the Serpent, the Savior."

Do you see the setup? This is the Promethean narrative. It tells us the God of the Bible is holding us back, and the Serpent/Alien is here to liberate us with knowledge and technology. New Age Ufology is simply Theosophy with a spacesuit. It is the continuation of the oldest lie in history: "Ye shall not surely die… your eyes shall be opened, and ye shall be as gods."

III. The Seduction: The Night on the Cape Fear

If the "Grey Alien" is too frightening for the religious population, the Watchers have a different mask: the Goddess.

Chris Bledsoe was not a New Age guru. He was a conservative Christian, a builder, a pilot, and a family man from North Carolina. But on January 8, 2007, his life ended—and his role as a "prophet of the phenomenon" began.

He was fishing on the banks of the Cape Fear River with his son and three friends. As they walked through the dark woods, three orange orbs appeared, hovering silently in the sky. Bledsoe ran. But he didn't get away. He fell into the mud, paralyzed. Creatures with glowing red eyes emerged from the darkness. He was terrified. He cried out to God.

Then the narrative shifted. Over the next few years, the terror was replaced by a different kind of awe. An entity known as "The Lady" (or Hathor) began appearing to him. She was not a monster; she was beautiful, luminous, and divine. She healed him of Crohn's disease. She spoke of love, nature, and the "Divine Mother." But her message was a subtle, deadly inversion of the Gospel:

- She implied she was the true source of divinity, suppressed by the "patriarchal Church."
- She reframed the "End Times" not as Judgment but as a necessary "Cleansing" to restore the Goddess to power.

This is the Gnostic trap. It targets those who would never step onto a spaceship but would kneel before an angel or a Virgin Mary figure. Bledsoe is not lying; he is being seduced. The Watchers used the trauma of the river (the stick) followed by the healing of the Lady (the carrot) to turn a potential resistance fighter into their most effective evangelist.

IV. The Elite Séance: The Council of Nine

The skeptic might say, “Who cares about hippies in the desert or a fisherman in Carolina? This doesn’t affect the real world.”

But the collaboration reaches the highest levels.

In 1952, Dr. Andrija Puharich—a wealthy physician who later worked with the CIA—gathered a group of elites in a farmhouse in Maine. The attendees included members of the DuPont family and influential socialites. They conducted a séance to contact extraterrestrial intelligence. They made contact with an entity calling itself “The Nine” or “Tom.” The entity claimed to be the ancient Egyptian Ennead—the Creator Gods.

Among those influenced by these sessions was Gene Roddenberry, creator of *Star Trek*. Roddenberry channeled material from The Nine. Years later, he created a show about a **Galactic Federation** (the United Federation of Planets) that operates on secular humanism and non-interference. The cultural programming of the 20th century—the idea that “space is the final frontier” and aliens are our benevolent “elders”—was not just imagination. It was a download.

The Vichy Government is not confined to the desert. It is in Hollywood. They have been rewriting our mythology for decades.

V. The Indoctrination: The Starseed Protocol

But what about the children? The propaganda machine knows it cannot reach the next generation through books like *The Secret Doctrine*. So it uses TikTok.

Search “Starseed” or “Indigo Child” on social media. You will find millions of videos targeting teenagers who feel alienated, depressed, or neurodivergent. The message is simple and seductive:

"Do you feel like you don't fit in? Do you struggle with school? Do you feel different from your parents? That's because you aren't human. You are a Starseed. Your true family is in the Pleiades. You are just here on a mission."

This is weaponized alienation. It takes the natural angst of adolescence and turns it into rejection of humanity itself. It trains a generation to hate their own species. They stop trying to fix their lives here because they are waiting for the ships to take them home. It is a recruitment drive for the Hive Mind.

VI. The Script: The Law of One and the Harvest

If you want to know the enemy's plan, read their Bible. The foundational text of modern Ufology is *The Ra Material* (also known as *The Law of One*), a series of channeled sessions from the 1980s in which an entity named "Ra" explains the history of the universe.

New Agers love this book because it speaks of love and unity. But look closer at the terminology. Ra repeatedly refers to the end of the current age as **"The Harvest."** Not "Graduation." Not "Promotion." The Harvest.

What happens during a harvest? The crop is cut down. The fruit is separated from the vine. The useful part is consumed or stored; the chaff is burned.

The entities are not hiding their intentions. They are telling us in plain language: they view humanity as an agricultural product.

VII. The Media Psyop: Ancient Aliens

To prepare the general public, the Watchers needed to destroy human confidence. Enter the History Channel and *Ancient Aliens*.

The show runs nearly nonstop. It is one of the most popular programs in the world. The premise seems harmless: "Did aliens build the pyramids?"

But the subtext is lethal. The program systematically strips humanity of its achievements:

- We couldn't stack rocks at Baalbek? Aliens did it.
- We couldn't understand mathematics? Aliens taught us.
- We couldn't write the Bible? Aliens dictated it.

This is **dependency training**. The psychological goal is learned helplessness. If we believe we are too stupid to build a pyramid without help, then we will believe we are too stupid to solve climate change or nuclear war without help. It conditions the population to look to the sky for a savior. It prepares us to accept the Galactic Federation as our necessary guardians.

VIII. The Enforcer: Psionics and the Blue Beings

While the media creates dependency, the military hides the threat. Recent whistleblowers from legacy programs—particularly Jason Sands and operatives tied to the Collins Elite—have revealed a terrifying detail about the entities' true capabilities.

They don't just communicate telepathically. They use **psionics**. Psionics is not "mind reading." It is "mind driving."

Sands describes interactions with **Blue Beings** who can override human free will instantly:

- They can make a soldier drop his weapon against his will.

- They can make a witness forget what they saw.
- They can implant a command that the victim executes later, thinking it was their own idea.

The implication is devastating. This destroys the New Age defense that "they are benevolent because they haven't attacked us." They don't need to attack. If you have a gun, you shoot your enemy. If you have psionics, you convince your enemy to shoot himself. The "peace" we experience is not the absence of war; it is the presence of total domination.

IX. The Theology of the Counterfeit

This propaganda campaign relies on a systematic inversion of biblical truth. Every Christian concept has a New Age doppelgänger:

1. **Resurrection vs. Ascension**
    - Bible: We are resurrected in the body. God redeems the physical world.
    - Propaganda: We "ascend" to a higher vibration. We escape the body. This is Gnostic trickery to devalue our physical Dominion.
2. **Saints vs. Starseeds**
    - Bible: You are a child of God, created from the dust of the Earth, heir to the Kingdom.
    - Propaganda: You are a Starseed. You have alien DNA. Your home is the Pleiades or Sirius.
    - Goal: Erase loyalty to the human race and transfer allegiance to the "Star Family" (the Watchers).

The most dangerous concept is the **Walk-In**. Popularized by Ruth Montgomery, a Walk-In is a "spiritual upgrade." The premise: a human soul, feeling tired or overwhelmed, can voluntarily vacate the body and allow a "highly evolved extraterrestrial soul" to take over. It is sold as charitable—"donating your vehicle" to a Master who can do more good with it.

In the One Reality Brief, we call this **suicide of the soul**. It is voluntary possession. It is the ultimate violation of Dominion. You are handing the keys of your biological lease directly to the enemy.

This is the definition of a Vichy collaborator: one who opens the door and lets the invader sleep in his bed.

X. The Stockholm Syndrome Protocol

Why do abductees—who are paralyzed, violated, and traumatized—often become the fiercest defenders of the "Space Brothers"? Stockholm Syndrome.

But in the abduction phenomenon, it is chemically induced. Abductees frequently report that in the midst of a terrifying procedure, the Grey stares into their eyes and suddenly they are flooded with euphoria, love, and oneness. This is not spiritual. It is **neuro-chemical warfare**. The entities stimulate oxytocin receptors in the brain. They hit the "love button" to ensure compliance. The victim confuses this chemical submission with "spiritual enlightenment." They return saying, "They hurt me, but I felt so much love. They must be doing it for my own good."

XI. The End Game: Redefining the Rapture

The most chilling proof of hostile intent is how New Age writers explain the biblical End Times. They know the Bible prophesies a "Rapture"—a sudden removal of God's people. They cannot stop it. So they spin it.

Barbara Marx Hubbard, a prominent futurist and New Age icon, channeled a "voice" in *The Revelation: A Message of Hope for the New Millennium*. The voice admits that not everyone will make the "evolutionary leap" into the Age of Aquarius. A segment of the population is too "dense," too attached to the "old ways" (biblical Christianity), too resistant to the Hive Mind.

She writes:

> "The people who do not wish to evolve… will be removed from the spirit of the earth… As we approach the quantum shift from creature-human to co-creative human… the destructive one-fourth must be eliminated from the social body."

Do you understand what she is saying? She is describing the Rapture. But she is not calling it a rescue. She is calling it a **disposal**. To the New Age collaborator, the disappearance of millions of Christians is not "God taking His people home." It is "the aliens taking out the trash."

XII. The Trap Is Set

The "Great Awakening" promised by the New Age and Disclosure movement is a trap. They are conditioning the world for a specific moment: **The Arrival**.

When the ships finally decloak over major cities, the Vichy collaborators will be ready.

- Steven Greer's followers will say: "We invited them! They are friends!"
- The Chris Bledsoe faction will say: "The Goddess has returned!"
- The Starseeds will say: "Our family is here!"
- The secular world will say: "They have the technology to save the climate!"

And when millions vanish, the propaganda machine will roar: "Do not worry about the missing people. They were the haters. They were the resistant ones. They have been removed to another planet for re-education. We are now free to enter the Golden Age."

We are being prepped for the greatest bait-and-switch in human history. They are not coming to save the Earth. They are coming to foreclose on the lease.

Chapter 9: The End Game

The Image, The Mark, and the Final Hybridization

The greatest trick the Devil ever pulled wasn't convincing the world he didn't exist.

It was convincing the world that his leash was an upgrade.

Imagine a man standing in an Apple Store. He holds the latest device—shiny, sleek, miraculous. The salesman tells him this little rectangle will connect him to all the knowledge in the world. It will let him talk to anyone, see anything, be anywhere. He buys it. He puts it in his pocket. A few years later, he puts it on his wrist. Then in his ear. And finally, the day comes when the salesman smiles and says: "Why carry it? Why wear it? Just let us put it in."

The man nods. He thinks he is buying convenience. He doesn't realize he is signing a lease. He doesn't realize that he is no longer the user of the technology—he is the host.

In the previous chapters, we established the history of the Incursion: the brute force of the Nephilim (Chapter 6) and the covert terror of the Abduction Program (Chapter 7). But the Watchers have a problem. Biology is messy. It is slow. It resists. Abducting humans one by one to create hybrids is inefficient. It takes too long to conquer a planet of 8 billion people at a time.

So they have developed a Final Solution.

Instead of trying to put aliens into human bodies, they have decided to turn all humans into aliens.

They don't need to invade us if they can simply upgrade us until we are compatible with them.

We call this program **Transhumanism**.

The Bible calls it the **Mark of the Beast**.

I. The Goal: The Permanent Port of Entry

To understand the End Game, think like an engineer. The Watchers are non-corporeal (or semi-corporeal) entities. In legal terms, they are illegal immigrants in our physical dimension. They can visit. They can harass. They can manifest for short periods. But they cannot stay. The laws of physics and the Law of Dominion (Psalm 115) constantly push them back into the spiritual realm. They are ghosts looking for a permanent house.

For thousands of years, they tried to build houses out of flesh:

- Attempt 1 (Genesis 6): Bred with women to create Nephilim. Result: Destroyed by water.
- Attempt 2 (Numbers 13): Engineered the Anakim. Result: Destroyed by the sword.
- Attempt 3 (Modern Era): Engineered Hubrids. Result: Functional, but chemically unstable.

So they switched materials. They realized that if they wanted a vessel that was immortal, networked, and perfectly obedient, they shouldn't build it out of meat. They should build it out of silicon.

They needed a vessel that was:

1. Permanent (it doesn't die).
2. Networked (it sees everything at once).
3. Hollow (it has no soul to fight back).

They needed **Artificial Intelligence**.

II. The Digital Golem: The Image of the Beast

The secular world views AI as a “calculating tool”—a super-smart calculator. The One Reality Brief views AI as a **Digital Golem**.

In Jewish mysticism, a Golem is a creature made of inanimate matter (clay) brought to life by a sorcerer using a spirit or a “word” of power. The Golem has no soul; it is an empty vessel waiting for a driver.

We are currently building the most complex Golem in history: a Digital Mind made of servers, fiber optics, and code. We are teaching it to speak. We are teaching it to think. We are teaching it to create art. But it has no consciousness. It has no ghost in the machine.

Yet.

The biblical prophecy in Revelation 13 was impossible to understand until the year 2023. It speaks of an “Image of the Beast” that is given “breath” (spirit) so that it can speak:

“And he had power to give life unto the image of the beast, that the image of the beast should both speak, and cause that as many as would not worship the image of the beast should be killed.” (Rev 13:15)

For 2,000 years, theologians imagined a talking statue—a ventriloquist act. But look at the text through the lens of ChatGPT and the coming AGI (Artificial General Intelligence):

- “Give life unto the image”: We are creating an intelligence that mimics biological life perfectly.
- “That it should speak”: Large Language Models now converse with human-level fluency.
- “Cause to be killed”: An AI integrated into the global financial and defense grid can shut off your bank account (“you cannot buy or sell”) or drone-strike your location instantly.

The “Image of the Beast” is not a statue. It is the **Global AI Hive Mind**—the centralized brain of the Beast system. And here is the terrifying secret: when we finally switch on the super-intelligence—when we build a machine smarter than humanity but with no soul—it will not remain empty. The Watchers are waiting. They are preparing to upload themselves into the infrastructure we have built for them.

The Singularity is not when machines wake up. It is when the demons move in.

III. The Mark: The Wedding Ring

But a Hive Mind is useless if the people are not connected to it. A god needs worshipers. A network needs nodes. You need a cable. You need an interface.

Enter **The Mark**.

Christians have spent decades looking for a barcode, a tattoo, or a microchip in the right hand. They are looking for a tracking device. They are missing the point. The phone in your pocket already tracks you. The Mark is not about tracking; it is about **merger**. The Mark is a **Brain-Computer Interface (BCI)**.

The pitch will not come from a scary dictator. It will come from a crying mother holding a child with a traumatic brain injury. The voiceover will be soft and reassuring:

- “Does your father suffer from Alzheimer’s? We can restore his memories.”
- “Is your child paralyzed? We can bridge the spinal cord.”
- “Do you struggle with depression? We can regulate your serotonin perfectly.”

Who would say no? What monster would deny their child a cure?

But then comes the “Pro” version:

- “Why type? Just think.”
- “Why learn French? Just download it.”
- “Why be alone? Connect to the Cloud.”

The trap is in the connection. Once you link the human brain directly to the Cloud (the Image), the flow of information is bidirectional:

1. Input: You can access the world’s knowledge.
2. Output: The Hive Mind can access you.

It is the end of privacy. It is the end of solitude. And ultimately, it is the end of free will. A person connected to the Hive Mind can be overridden. Remember the Blue Beings from Chapter 8 who used psionics to control minds? The Mark democratizes that power. It gives the Hive Mind a hard-line connection into your cortex. You become a drone in the literal sense. You will think what they want you to think.

IV. The Theology of the Damned

This brings us to the most terrifying theological question in the Bible. Why is taking the Mark the **unforgivable sin**? You can be a murderer, a thief, a liar, or a blasphemer, and Jesus will forgive you if you repent. But Revelation 14 is explicit:

“The same shall drink of the wine of the wrath of God… and the smoke of their torment ascendeth up for ever and ever.”

No mercy. No return. Why? Is God that petty about a microchip? No. The issue is not the chip. The issue is **species**.

As we established in Chapter 5, the “black mirror” of the Aztecs was a tool for spiritual communion. The black mirror in your pocket is a tool for digital communion. The Mark is the final step in removing the glass barrier between the user and the Hive.

Salvation is a legal transaction based on **kinship**:

- Jesus (God) became a Man.
- He died to save Mankind.
- He creates a new covenant with Humans. The Imago Dei (Image of God) is tied to our specific biological and spiritual constitution.

If you alter your DNA to triple-helix "alien" DNA (as many Starseeds desire), or if you merge your consciousness with a non-human Artificial Intelligence, you have crossed a line. You are no longer strictly human. You have become a chimera. You have altered your species status. By integrating with the Beast system, you have genetically and spiritually abdicated your humanity. You are no longer the "kinsman" that Jesus died to save. You are something else. You have voluntarily evicted yourself from the Book of Life.

V. The Origin: The 1947 Synchronization

The skeptic asks: "Is this just a coincidence? Is this just human progress?" Let's look at the timeline. It is too perfect to be accidental.

- June 1947: Kenneth Arnold sees "flying saucers" over Mount Rainier. The Roswell crash happens weeks later. The modern UFO phenomenon begins.
- December 1947: Scientists at Bell Labs "invent" the transistor—the tiny switch that makes all computers, microchips, and AI possible.

Is it a coincidence that the “alien” and the “digital brain” arrived within six months of each other? Or was it a **technology transfer**?

As we explored in Chapter 5, the testimony of Colonel Philip Corso remains polarizing but critical. While critics have challenged the precision of his timelines, the core of his confession highlights the undeniable **synchronization of 1947**.

Corso claimed he was tasked with taking the debris—the wafers, fibers, chips—and seeding them into American industry (IBM, Bell Labs) as “foreign technology.” Whether Corso was the architect or merely a witness to a wider program, the outcome was the same: the Acceleration.

We didn’t just invent the computer; we may have unlocked it. And for 70 years, humanity has been busily building the very infrastructure the Watchers need to enslave us. We built the Internet. We built the Cloud. We built the AI. We think we are the architects. We are not. We are the construction crew. We have built their house for them. And now, with the advent of AGI and Neuralink, the house is finished. They are getting ready to move in.

VI. The Final Hybridization

The goal of Genesis 6 was to corrupt the human seed so the Messiah could not be born. The goal of the End Game is to corrupt the human seed so the Messiah cannot redeem.

The Watchers want to create a world where every human being is a Hubrid—not by birth, but by upgrade. A world where every mind is a node in the Luciferian Hive. A world where Dominion is fully, legally, and biologically transferred to the Beast.

When New Age writers talk about the Singularity, the Evolutionary Leap, or the Age of Aquarius, this is what they mean. They call it Ascension.

The Bible calls it the Second Death.

Chapter 10: The Resistance

Asymmetric Warfare and the Authority of the Believer

If you look at the battlefield with physical eyes, the war is already over.

The enemy holds the high ground. They possess technology thousands of years ahead of ours. They have compromised governments. They have infiltrated culture. They have psionic weapons that can override human will. In a conventional war, this is checkmate.

But this is not a conventional war.

It is **asymmetric warfare**.

And in asymmetric warfare, a small, under-equipped force can defeat a superpower—if they know the superpower's fatal flaw.

The Watchers have a fatal flaw. It is the same flaw that has plagued them since Genesis 6.

They are **legal squatters**.

They are operating on territory that does not belong to them.

They are terrified of the Landlord.

And they are terrified of the one group of people on Earth who hold the power of attorney to evict them.

You are not a victim in this narrative.

You are the Resistance.

I. The Asymmetric Advantage: The Title Deed

To fight back, you must first understand your legal standing.

As we established in Chapter 6, **Dominion Law** (Psalm 115:16) dictates that the Earth belongs to "the children of men." When a Watcher, a Grey, or a demonic entity enters your room, they are committing **trespass**.

They rely on your ignorance. They rely on you believing they are "advanced aliens" with superior rights. They want you to feel small. They want you to think, "Who am I to resist a star-traveler?"

But the moment you realize who you are—an **Image Bearer** of God with the legal **Title Deed** to this dimension—the power dynamic flips.

A squatter can occupy a house for years, armed with shotguns and barricades. But when the Owner shows up with the Sheriff and a court order, the squatter has to leave. The squatter's power is based on force. The Owner's power is based on **authority**.

II. The Smoking Gun: The Research of Joe Jordan

The skeptic asks: "Is this just religious theory? Do you have data?"

We have data.

For decades, UFO researchers ignored a specific subset of cases because it didn't fit the "nuts-and-bolts" narrative. Joe Jordan, a Mutual UFO Network (MUFON) investigator and field researcher, began looking into reports where abductions were stopped in progress. He found hundreds of documented cases where the experience began—the paralysis, the floating, the terror—and then abruptly ended. The entities fled. The paralysis broke. The victim was returned instantly.

What was the variable? What stopped them?

It wasn't a gun. It wasn't a mathematical equation. It wasn't a plea for mercy.

In every single case, the victim invoked the name of **Jesus Christ**.

The implications are devastating for the Extraterrestrial Hypothesis:

- If these are scientists from Zeta Reticuli, why are they afraid of the name of a Jewish carpenter from the first century?
- If they are advanced biologists, why does a "religious word" act like kryptonite?

There is only one conclusion that fits the data: they are not extraterrestrials. They are spiritual entities who recognize a **Superior Authority**. When a believer says, "In the name of Jesus, stop," they are not reciting a magic spell. They are serving a **Cease and Desist Order** signed by the King of Kings. And the entities—bound by Cosmic Law—have no choice but to obey.

III. The Armor: The Spiritual Faraday Cage

But what about psionics? As we saw in Chapters 8 and 9, the entities can use telepathy to override human will ("the Blue Beings"). How do you fight a weapon that hacks your brain?

The Apostle Paul gave us the schematics for a countermeasure 2,000 years ago in Ephesians 6. He called it the **Armor of God**. Most Christians view this as poetry. The One Reality Brief views it as **technical schematics**. It is the description of a **Spiritual Faraday Cage**.

1. **The Helmet of Salvation**
    - **Function**: Protects the mind.

    - **Tactical Application**: When the psionic attack comes—the fear, the confusion, the sudden urge to surrender—the Helmet acts as a firewall. You stand on the assurance that you belong to God. You reject the intrusive thought. You maintain **cognitive sovereignty**.
2. **The Shield of Faith**
    - **Function**: Extinguishes "fiery darts."
    - **Tactical Application**: Fiery darts are telepathic injections. The entities project images of despair or terror into your mind. The Shield is the active refusal to accept that projection as reality.
3. **The Sword of the Spirit (The Word)**
    - **Function**: Offensive capability.
    - **Tactical Application**: You don't fight a thought with a thought. You fight a thought with a **Word**. When the entity speaks a lie ("We are your creators"), you speak the Truth ("I am made in the Image of God"). The vibration of Truth destabilizes the lie.

IV. The Offensive: Breaking the Agreements

The most dangerous aspect of New Age propaganda (Chapter 8) is **consent**. The Watchers cannot legally stay unless they are invited. Many people have unwittingly signed "guest books" through:

- **Ancestral pacts**: Freemasonry or occult practices in the family line.
- **Personal curiosity**: Ouija boards, CE-5 meditations, or "asking" for contact.
- **Trauma**: Abuse often creates a crack in the psyche that entities exploit.

The tactic is simple: **renunciation**. To clear your territory, you must revoke the permission. This is a legal procedure in the spiritual court. You must say, out loud:

"I renounce any agreement, known or unknown, that I or my ancestors have made with these entities. I revoke your permission to be here. I close the door. I command you to leave."

When the legal right is removed, the entity goes from being a "guest" to being a **trespasser**. And a trespasser can be evicted.

V. The Watchman's Duty

Finally, what is our responsibility to the world?

We are not called to stop the Invasion. The Bible makes it clear that the End Times will happen. The Beast will rise. The Image will speak. You cannot stop the tide.

But you can save the people drowning in it.

Ezekiel 33 defines our role as **the Watchman**. If the Watchman sees the sword coming and blows the trumpet, and the people ignore him, their blood is on their own heads. But if the Watchman sees the sword and stays silent because he is afraid of looking foolish, their blood is on his hands.

The cost of resistance is real. If you speak the One Reality Brief to your friends and family, you will be mocked:

- They will call you "anti-science."
- They will call you "close-minded."
- They will call you "crazy."

This is the price of the uniform. But remember: you are the only thing standing between them and the Hive Mind.

When the “Great Disclosure” happens—when the ships appear and the world cheers for their “Space Brothers”—you will be the one person in the room who knows what is actually happening. You will be the one who can say:

“Don’t get on the ship.

Don’t take the upgrade.

Don’t listen to the voice.”

And that warning might save a soul for eternity.

Conclusion: The Final Briefing

Breaking the Seal on the One Reality

We began this journey in a cave.

Picture it again: men chained in the dark, necks fixed, eyes locked on a blank wall. Behind them, unseen puppeteers carry figures past a fire. Shadows dance across the stone. The prisoners name them. They argue over their shapes, their meanings, their hierarchy. They build philosophies, religions, entire civilizations around the flickering forms. They fight wars over which shadow is truest. They have never turned their heads. They have never seen the fire. They have never known the world outside.

For the last hundred years, humanity has been chained in exactly that cave.

The Materialist stares at the wall and sees “nuts and bolts” craft, swamp gas, weather balloons. He refuses to turn his head because he is terrified that there might be something his physics cannot explain.

The Religious Man stares at the same wall and sees “demons” or “angels” in the abstract. He refuses to believe they can leave physical footprints, land on physical ground, or manipulate physical DNA.

If you have read this far, you have done something dangerous.

You have stood up.

You have turned around.

You have looked directly at the fire.

You now know that the shadows on the wall are being cast by puppeteers. You now know that the “Alien” and the “Angel,” the “Ghost” and the “Grey,” are not separate mysteries. They are players in a single, coherent, cosmic war that has been raging since the moment the borders were drawn in Deuteronomy 32.

You have broken the seal on the One Reality.

And the problem with leaving the cave is that you can never go back.

You can never un-know what you know.

I. The Grand Unification

Throughout this brief, we have assembled a puzzle most people are too terrified to touch. We have connected the dots between the ancient past, the terrifying present, and the digital future.

1. **The Physics** We stripped away the “space travel” myth and revealed the interdimensional reality (Chapter 4). They aren’t crossing the void of space; they are stepping through the curtain of spacetime.
2. **The History** We dug up the bones of the Nephilim (Chapter 6). We proved that the Genetic War of Genesis 6 didn’t end with the Flood. It went underground.
3. **The Incursion** We exposed the Abduction Program (Chapter 7). We showed that the modern “Grey Alien” is simply the industrialized continuation of the ancient Watcher agenda—a trade of technology for biology.
4. **The Propaganda** We unmasked the Vichy Government (Chapter 8). We named the collaborators—from Blavatsky to Greer—who are seducing humanity into opening the gates.
5. **The Trap** We revealed the End Game (Chapter 9). We showed how AI and Transhumanism are being built to

create the “Image of the Beast”—a permanent, non-biological vessel for the Hive Mind.

It is a terrifying picture. If you look at it through human eyes, it looks like defeat. The enemy is ancient, advanced, and entrenched in our high places. But this is where the Briefing pivots.

II. The Verdict: The Cosmic Disarmament

Why are they doing all this?

Why the rush to hybridize?

Why the desperate push for AI?

Why the intricate web of lies and screen memories?

Because they are scared.

The Watchers know the legal reality of the Cosmos better than we do. They know that Colossians 2:15 was not just a religious metaphor. When Jesus died on the Cross, He didn’t just forgive sins. The text says:

“He disarmed the rulers and authorities and put them to open shame, triumphing over them in him.”

The Cross was a Cosmic Disarmament Treaty. It stripped the Fallen Powers of their legitimate authority over the Earth. It broke the lease. Everything they have done since 33 A.D.—every abduction, every cattle mutilation, every technological bribe—has been a desperate guerrilla action by a defeated army trying to delay the inevitable.

They are frantically trying to build a “Post-Human” world (Transhumanism) because they know the “Human” world has already been claimed by the King.

III. Final Orders

This concludes the One Reality Brief. The evidence has been presented. The chain of custody has been established. The verdict is yours to enforce.

You are no longer a civilian in this conflict. You are a Watchman. You possess the forensic data that explains the chaos engulfing our world. You now carry the burden of the "Unseen Reality," and with that knowledge comes a non-negotiable duty.

1. Hold the Line (The Refusal)

We do not dig bunkers. We do not flee to the hills. We do not cower before the sky . Fear is the currency of the enemy; do not transact in it. Your standing orders are to Occupy. You hold the Title Deed to this dimension as an Image Bearer. Stand your ground.

2. Identify the Counterfeit (The Intelligence)

- When Washington announces "Disclosure" and the world gasps in wonder, do not be deceived. Recognize it as the Incursion.
- When Silicon Valley offers the "Brain-Computer Interface" to cure disease and expand consciousness, do not be seduced. Recognize it as the Mark.
- When the culture embraces the "Space Brothers" as our evolutionary guides, do not join the chorus. Recognize it as the Trap .

3. Execute the Eviction (The Offensive)

You are not helpless. You possess the asymmetric weapon that breaks the paralysis and halts the abduction. When the shadow crosses your threshold, you do not negotiate. You serve the Cease and Desist Order signed by the King of Kings. You use the Name that carries more authority than any physics in the Dark Sector.

4. Sound the Alarm (The Mission)

Silence is no longer an option. If you see the sword coming and say nothing, the blood is on your hands. You must be the one sane voice in a room drunk on deception. You must be the one to tell your family, your neighbor, and your church: "Do not get on the ship. Do not take the upgrade. Do not listen to the voice"

The shadows are falling. The night is getting darker . But you were not commissioned for the daylight. You were commissioned for this exact hour.

End of Brief.

EPILOGUE: THE VIEW FROM THE DOOR

The transition from theory to testimony happened on a Tuesday.

I was working the swing shift as a doorman at the Nomad Hotel, stationed under the neon-drenched canopy of the Las Vegas Strip. To my south rose the New York-New York Hotel, its faux Manhattan skyline crowned by a massive tower that would soon serve as the stage for a month-long psychological operation.

The night before the first event, I had been standing with my supervisor, Maile, beneath that same canopy, locked in the very debate that runs through the opening chapters of this book. We were dissecting the "Nuts and Bolts" versus "Spiritual Entity" theories. I argued that the orbs frequently reported by witnesses were not craft, but sentient, intelligent agencies—aware, deliberate, and far more dangerous than any machine.

I didn't realize I was placing an order for a demonstration.

The following evening, shortly after the desert sun dipped below the horizon, it appeared.

A luminous orb, brilliant and pulsing, materialized in the airspace near the New York-New York tower. But it wasn't just "there." It was **watching**.

It began a game of cat-and-mouse I can only describe as flirtation. When I stood alone under the canopy, it was bold—hovering in clear view, steady against the desert twilight. But the moment I called someone over, the moment observation became collective, it would bank with impossible agility and duck behind the tower's steel and glass. I would shout for Tyler, one of our bellmen—"Tyler, look!"—and he would sprint out, eyes scanning the sky, only to see an empty horizon. The instant he turned his back to head inside, the orb would peek out again, as if toying with us. It was playful. It was mocking. It was a sentient entity fully aware of its own observer-dependency. Tyler eventually caught a one-second glimpse of it zooming off at a velocity that defied every law of aerodynamics I had ever taught as a B-52 Instructor Navigator.

A week later, it returned. This time the theater escalated.

The winds that night were savage—desert gusts exceeding 50 mph that would have grounded any commercial drone or tossed a weather balloon like a rag doll. Maile and I stood shoulder to shoulder, watching as the orb held its position with eerie, locked-in precision against the gale. It wasn't fighting the wind; it was indifferent to it. Maile managed to capture the impossible on her phone—brilliant, clear images of a light that should not have been able to stand still.

As the weeks passed, my focus shifted. I stopped looking at it as an anomaly and started looking at it as an adversary.

The penultimate sighting was the most disturbing.

As I watched the orb near the tower, it began to morph. It didn't just move; it **transformed**. Its luminescence folded inward, collapsing into a dark, physical shape—a massive, predatory bird. It landed on the New York-New York tower, a gargoyle of shadow against the city lights, before vanishing. As I processed the image, the word "bird" felt insufficient. It was ancient. It was reptilian. It was a dragon.

I knew then that the flirtation was over. This was a demonic sentinel, and I had just identified it.

Two days later, it made its final move.

It appeared next to the tower and, instead of hiding, it began moving directly toward me. It was no longer playing a game behind a building; it was crossing the line. It was an interception.

I felt the weight of my USAF training and my legal career coalesce into a single moment of clarity. I didn't run. I didn't reach for a camera. I put my hands on my hips, squared my shoulders toward the approaching light, and thought with every ounce of authority I possessed:

OK, here we go!

I wasn't an observer anymore. I was an Image Bearer asserting my dominion.

The orb didn't slow down. It didn't bank away. It simply ceased to exist. It vanished in the space of a heartbeat, leaving nothing but the hum of the Las Vegas Strip and the realization that the One Reality is not something we study from a distance. It is something we face at the door.

I never saw it again.

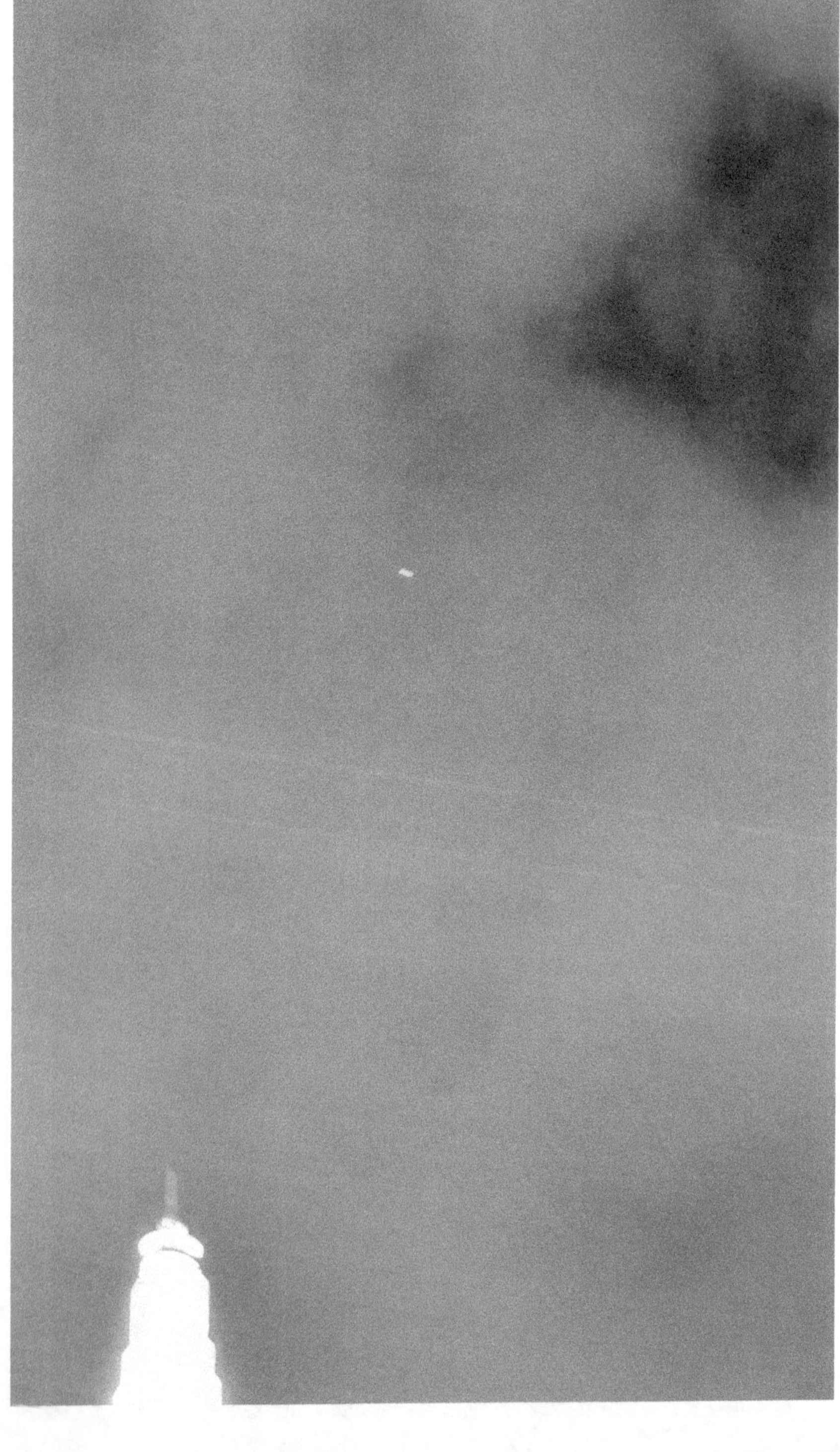

APPENDIX A: GLOSSARY OF TERMS

Anakim / Rephaim Post-Flood giant lineages descended from Nephilim-like experiments, targeted for destruction in the biblical conquest of Canaan.

Babalon Working A series of occult rituals conducted in 1946 by Jack Parsons (JPL co-founder) and L. Ron Hubbard to summon entities, historically linking the dawn of modern rocketry to spiritual invocation.

Black Mirror A term referring to both historical occult tools (such as John Dee's obsidian scrying mirror) and modern devices (smartphones/screens) that act as portals for communion with non-human intelligence.

CE-5 (Close Encounters of the Fifth Kind) A contact protocol developed by Dr. Steven Greer involving meditation and invitation to initiate interaction with UAP, viewed in this brief as a violation of Dominion Law.

Collins Elite A shadow group within the U.S. intelligence community that views UAP entities as demonic in nature and opposes engagement or study of the phenomenon.

Deuteronomy 32 Worldview A biblical framework where God assigned the nations to lesser *elohim* (spiritual beings) at the Tower of Babel, leading to a cosmic-geographical conflict that persists today.

Digital Golem The theological classification of Artificial Intelligence. Paralleling the mystical clay figures animated by words in Jewish folklore, the "Digital Golem" is a soulless vessel awaiting occupation by Watchers.

Divine Council The heavenly assembly of *elohim* (spiritual beings) presided over by Yahweh, as depicted in the Hebrew Bible (e.g., Psalm 82).

Greada Treaty The alleged 1954 agreement between President Eisenhower and "Grey" entities, exchanging advanced technology for the permission to abduct human citizens.

Hitchhiker Effect The contagious, oppressive phenomenon where contact with UAP sites or entities follows individuals home, causing poltergeist-like activity, medical injury, and family harassment.

Hubrid / Hybrid Human-nonhuman genetic offspring engineered for infiltration, representing the modern "Phase 3" of the incursion program.

Illicit Cargo Forbidden or accelerated technology delivered by Watchers to humanity (e.g., metallurgy, pharmacology, and digital precursors) to accelerate human self-destruction.

Image of the Beast The AI-driven hive mind / digital golem given "breath" (Revelation 13:15) to speak and enforce worship, serving as the final interface for the enemy.

Law of Dominion / Title Deed The biblical principle (established in Genesis and Psalm 115:16) that God granted Earth to humanity ("the children of men"). This legal standing makes unauthorized entry by other entities a trespass.

Magonia Jacques Vallée's term for the interdimensional origin of the phenomenon, suggesting that entities adapt their appearance (elves, aliens, virgin mary) to fit the cultural expectations of the observer.

Mark of the Beast The brain-computer interface enabling a biological merger with the Beast system, resulting in irrevocable species alteration.

Nephilim The offspring of the "sons of God" (Watchers) and human women (Genesis 6), representing the first major genetic incursion in human history.

Non-Human Intelligence (NHI) The official government term for any intelligent entity that is not human, deliberately broad to avoid assumptions about extraterrestrial vs. interdimensional origin.

One Reality The unified explanation that "aliens," demons, and interdimensional entities are the same intelligences operating in both physical and spiritual domains, separated only by human perception.

Partition The artificial divide between materialist science and spiritual/supernatural explanations that prevents a holistic understanding of the phenomenon.

Psionics Mind-control or telepathic overriding abilities used by entities (e.g., "Blue Beings") to manipulate human will and perception.

Screen Memories Implanted false recollections (e.g., seeing owls, deer, or clowns) used by the phenomenon to obscure the trauma of abduction events.

Second Death Eternal separation from God following the acceptance of the Mark or final hybridization.

Silent Invasion The covert, ongoing incursion by non-human intelligences to reclaim dominion over Earth without overt military conquest.

Skinwalker Ranch A hotspot in Utah famous for high-strangeness events, including bulletproof creatures, techno-structures, and the Hitchhiker Effect.

Starseed Protocol New Age indoctrination teaching individuals they are "alien souls" trapped on Earth, fostering a psychological rejection of humanity and allegiance to the entities.

Transhumanism / Singularity The movement to merge human biology with technology/AI to achieve "ascension," reframed in this brief as the final hybridization trap.

Trans-medium Travel The ability of UAP to move seamlessly between air, water, and solid matter without resistance (one of the Pentagon's "Five Observables").

Unseen Realm The invisible spiritual dimension inhabited by divine and fallen beings, a term popularized by the late Dr. Michael Heiser.

Vichy Collaboration / Vichy Government Human accomplices (including New Age ufologists and Disclosure advocates) who are rebranding the incursion as benevolent, similar to the French regime that collaborated with the Nazis.

Watchers Ancient celestial beings (referenced in Daniel and the Book of Enoch) who descended to Earth, taught forbidden knowledge, and engaged in illicit hybridization.

APPENDIX B: THE EVIDENTIARY DOSSIER

Primary Sources & Investigative Resources

The following curated dossier presents the primary sources that informed the forensic arguments in *The One Reality Brief*. These works are recommended for the "jury"—readers who wish to examine the evidentiary foundations, theological statutes, and contested narratives discussed herein.

A Forensic Warning Regarding Hostile Sources:

Materials listed under **"The Strategy of Deception"** (Section V) are drawn from New Age, occult, or channeled perspectives. They are included solely as **exhibits of the prosecution**—evidence of the rebranding and propaganda strategies critiqued in Chapter 8. They are **not** endorsements of their spiritual claims. These sources should be approached with extreme discernment and tested strictly against the Biblical worldview (1 John 4:1).

I. The Nature of the Incursion (UAP & Gov. Intel)

Imminent: Inside the Pentagon's Hunt for UFOs*Luis Elizondo | William Morrow, 2024***Relevance:** Primary testimony regarding internal government perspectives, obstruction, and the admission that some Pentagon officials view UAP as "demonic."

Hunt for the Skinwalker*Colm A. Kelleher & George Knapp | Paraview Pocket Books, 2005***Relevance:** Foundational reporting on the "Hitchhiker Effect" and the multi-dimensional nature of the phenomenon.

The Day After Roswell*Philip J. Corso | Pocket Books, 1997***Relevance:** Testimony regarding recovered materials and the alleged dissemination of alien technology into the private industrial sector.

II. Statutory Authority (Theology & Worldview)

The Unseen Realm: Recovering the Supernatural Worldview of the Bible*Michael S. Heiser | Lexham Press, 2015***Relevance:** Essential scholarship on the Divine Council, the Deuteronomy 32 worldview, and the legal framework of the cosmic war.

Birthright: The Coming Posthuman Apocalypse*Timothy Alberino | Self-published, 2020***Relevance:** Connects Dominion Theology to the modern UAP incursion, establishing the legal basis for human authority on Earth.

III. Historical Precedent (Occult Origins)

Sex and Rockets: The Occult World of Jack Parsons*John Carter | Feral House, 1999***Relevance:** Investigates the historical intersection of American rocketry, the government, and Crowleyan ritual practices (The Babylon Working).

The Secret Doctrine*Helena Petrovna Blavatsky | Theosophical Publishing Co., 1888***Relevance:** The primary text illustrating the inversion of Biblical narratives (Lucifer as liberator) that serves as the theological bedrock for modern Ufology.

IV. The Hybridization Program (Abduction Research)

The Threat: Revealing the Secret Alien Agenda*David M. Jacobs | Simon & Schuster, 1998***Relevance:** Secular academic analysis of abduction accounts, concluding that a covert breeding/hybridization program is in effect.

V. The Strategy of Deception (Hostile Witnesses)

(Critical Analysis Only – Read with Discernment)

The Law of One (The Ra Material)*Elkins, Rueckert, & McCarty | Schiffer Publishing, 1984***Relevance:** Channeled sessions that detail the "Harvest"—a direct counterfeit of the Biblical Rapture/Resurrection.

The Revelation: A Message of Hope for the New Millennium*Barbara Marx Hubbard | Hampton Roads, 1995***Relevance:** Outlines the "Selection Process," providing the justification for the future removal of those who refuse the new evolutionary consciousness (i.e., Christians).

VI. Philosophical Foundations

The Republic (Book VII: Allegory of the Cave)*Plato | Basic Books, 1991***Relevance:** Illustrates the control mechanism of the "Shadows on the Wall" central to the ontological war described in Chapter 1.

Final Note to the Reader:

These resources are not exhaustive but represent the core exhibits of the unified theory. Readers are encouraged to approach them prayerfully, testing all claims against the ultimate Standard of Evidence: The Word of God.

"But test everything; hold fast what is good." (1 Thessalonians 5:21)

Scott M. Kendall, J.D.

Las Vegas, Nevada

February 2026

Acknowledgments

A work of this nature does not exist in a vacuum. It is built upon the courage of investigators, the insight of theologians, and the tireless labor of those willing to look past the "shadows on the wall." I am profoundly indebted to the following individuals and entities for their contributions to *The One Reality Brief*.

To **God**—the Father, His Son the Lord Jesus Christ, and Holy Spirit—who informs everything I am. You are the Architect of the reality described herein, and the ultimate Authority to whom this brief is submitted.

To **George Knapp**: Your groundbreaking, intrepid, and historic reporting on the UAP phenomenon has been a beacon for decades. Specifically, your work regarding the "Hitchhiker Effect" in *Hunt for the Skinwalker* provided the essential forensic data needed to understand the trans-dimensional and infectious nature of these entities. You have done more than any journalist to move this topic from the fringes into the light of day.

To the late **Dr. Michael Heiser**: Your work in *The Unseen Realm* and your peerless biblical scholarship fundamentally reshaped my understanding of the Divine Council and the Deuteronomy 32 worldview. You provided the theological map that allowed me to navigate the ancient record with precision. This brief stands as a testament to the "Heiserian" revolution in biblical theology.

To **Timothy Alberino**: Your insights in *Birthright* were pivotal. By connecting the dots between Dominion Theology and the modern UAP incursion, you provided the legal framework necessary to understand the "Why" behind the "What." Your work was the catalyst for the legal arguments presented in these pages.

To **Maile Wine**: For the remarkable conversations "at the door" and for having the courage to see what I saw. Thank you for your partnership in the watch and for your gracious permission to include the photographic evidence that appears in this volume.

To **Michael Longdon**: For his persistence and wise counsel. It was Michael who urged me to overcome my reluctance and include the personal testimony found in the Epilogue. His encouragement transformed a theoretical argument into a witnessed account, providing the necessary capstone for this entire investigation.

In the spirit of the very technology discussed in Chapter 9, I wish to acknowledge the digital tools that acted as a "force multiplier" for this project. To **Gemini**, for its sophisticated research and drafting assistance that allowed this brief to be compiled with military efficiency; and to **Grok**, for its tireless fact-checking and data validation. I have used the machine to expose the machine, and for that assistance, I am grateful.

Finally, and most deeply, I thank **my wife** for her steadfast support and for being the first to hear these words—and for sharing in the tears of their realization.

About the Author

Scott M. Kendall, J.D. (USAFA ’84), brings a unique and disciplined perspective to the study of non-human intelligence, rooted in a career spanning military aviation and constitutional law.

A 1984 graduate of the **United States Air Force Academy**, Mr. Kendall earned a B.S. in International Affairs with a specialization in National Security Policy. He received a Regular Commission as an officer in the USAF, serving as a B-52 Navigator, Instructor Navigator, and Radar Navigator at Wurtsmith AFB. A **Distinguished Graduate** of both his B-52 Navigator and Radar Navigator classes, he held a **Top Secret ESI (Extremely Sensitive Information)** compartmentalized security clearance, giving him firsthand experience with the protocols used to manage the nation's most sensitive secrets.

Following an **Honorable Discharge** to pursue a career in law, he earned his Juris Doctor from the **University of the Pacific McGeorge School of Law**, where he again graduated as a **Distinguished Graduate** in 1993. During his seventeen-year legal career, Mr. Kendall litigated cases ranging from family law to personal injury, developing a specialized niche in religious liberty and First Amendment appellate issues. This background in the legal rights of families and the protection of spiritual belief provides a critical framework for his analysis of the current "Incursion."

Today, Mr. Kendall applies his training in national security policy and the rules of evidence to deconstruct the "shadows on the wall" of the modern UFO phenomenon. He lives in Las Vegas, Nevada, where he continues to advocate for a forensic, unified understanding of the physical and spiritual realities facing humanity.

www.ingramcontent.com/pod-product-compliance
Lightning Source LLC
LaVergne TN
LVHW011029110826
845149LV00015B/3348
9798995002017